THE TEACHING OF AMERICAN HISTORY IN HIGH SCHOOLS

THE TEACHING OF AMERICAN HISTORY IN HIGH SCHOOLS

BY
MAURICE G. BAXTER
ROBERT H. FERRELL
JOHN E. WILTZ

INDIANA UNIVERSITY PRESS / BLOOMINGTON

CONTENTS

★ | # FOREWORD

On a recent trip abroad, one of the authors of this volume was visiting the palace of Versailles where he had a conversation with an American student. The student and a friend were looking at one of the palace exhibits which happened to be the Quai d'Orsay copy of the Treaty of Alliance of 1778 between the United States and France—the most important treaty in American history.

"What's that?" said the student's friend.

"Well," answered the student, "that's a treaty ending the war between England and France that began somewhere about that time, you know, about 1757. The war ended in 1759 but they didn't sign the treaty for some years afterward."

"Listen," I interrupted diplomatically, "that is the Treaty of Alliance of 1778, the most famous treaty in American history."

"I don't think so," replied the student. "That's the treaty ending the war of 1757."

"Well, it isn't," was the answer, "and I happen to have studied that subject."

The student looked slightly abashed, but not much.

"Are you a college student?" I asked.

"Yes," was the reply. "This fall I enter Harvard."

The present volume is a result of the Lilly Program in American History at Indiana University in Bloomington, where with two large subventions from the Lilly Endowment, Inc., of Indianapolis the department of history has conducted a program for high school teachers of American history throughout the state. The program began when several members of the department decided that they had talked long enough about the need for the university's historians to assist the state's teachers, and discovered not merely the concern but received the extraordinarily generous support of the Lilly Endowment. The initial idea was to bring several score of teachers of high school American history to the university where they could study in the department for three successive summers, doing guided reading in the intervals between summer school, and receive thereby an M.A. or M.A.T. (Master of Arts for Teachers) degree in history. The Endowment underwrote tuition and expenses of the Lilly fellows. At the present time over a hundred teachers have entered the program. There were other ideas which the Endowment has supported into practice—members of the university's history department have visited public and private high schools and junior high schools around the state, and the department has set up a summer off-campus reading program of paperbacked books under which students obtain graduate history credit. The program is publishing John E. Wiltz, *Books in American History: A Basic List for High Schools* (Indiana University Press, 1964; $1.00).

The Teaching of American History in High Schools has its own rather special background. It bases itself on the authors' experiences in schools about the state; on close contacts with Lilly fellows; on over 200 interviews (mostly taped) with fellows and other teachers; and on detailed questionnaires sent to all the state's high school librarians and, especially, to every teacher of high school American history in the state. We have included the results of the questionnaires in Chapter 7 of this book. The six preceding chapters represent our own opinions, at least in their recommendations, but we have based these chapters on our photograph, so to speak, of the teaching of American history in the state—the picture constructed from experience, interviews, and questionnaires.

We would like to express our heartfelt appreciation and thanks to the Lilly Endowment, Inc., and to its present director for education, Kenneth S. Templeton (and to his predecessor Manning M. Pattillo), for innumerable courtesies and helpfulness. It has been a great pleasure to work with such friends.

We are of course indebted to many individuals at Bloomington. John T. Liell has been an expert guide in construction of the questionnaires and in their mysterious routing through the electronic machine; we have much admired and benefited from his shrewdness and professional skill. We stand in debt to department colleagues, some of whom have been active in the Lilly program: Victor M. Bogle, Robert F. Byrnes, Donald F. Carmony (former director of the program), H. Trevor Colbourn, Shirley Engle, Charles Leonard Lundin, John P. Lunstrum, Chase C. Mooney (visiting professor in the program), Walter T. K. Nugent, Göran Rystad, George Soulis, Gerald Strauss, Rena Vassar (visiting professor), Oscar O. Winther (visiting professor). Some of these colleagues, we must add, do not agree with our conclusions in every particular, or even our photograph of the situation. We wish also to thank the graduate student members—mostly former high school teachers of American history—of a seminar held to discuss the chapters of this book: Robert Britton, Robert Feldman, Richard McKinzie, Carol Marion, Kathleen O'Connor, Ronald H. Ridgley, Eugene Trani, Harold Lew Wallace, Theodore A. Wilson. And to thank our skilled research assistants: Marilec Kindschi, Meridel Scherer Rawlins, Jeannette Schershel, Pauline Willis. Finally, we want to acknowledge the fine editorial work of Jane Rodman of the Indiana University Press.

As for responsibility for the following chapters: John E. Wiltz wrote Chapters One and Two; Maurice G. Baxter, Three and Five; Robert H. Ferrell, Four and Six; John E. Wiltz and Maurice G. Baxter combined to do Chapter Seven.

M.G.B.

R.H.F.

J.E.W.

Bloomington, Indiana

THE TEACHING OF AMERICAN HISTORY IN HIGH SCHOOLS

1 | THE TEACHER

Whenever one visits schools in Indiana—from the steel mill and prairie areas of the north, to the hill counties along the Ohio River—he will find some people expressing deep concern over the high school course in American history. Although the present era often reserves its largest enthusiasm for science and technology, perceptive administrators, teachers, parents, and civic leaders recognize that in this age when the achievements of the physicist and mathematician threaten man's existence, the humanities and social sciences (in high schools rather loosely called "social studies") have assumed new importance. They realize that man's sur-

15

vival may depend upon knowledge of sociology and government, economics and history, literature and the arts. They realize that many of today's problems are beyond the capacity of natural science to resolve, that human welfare and happiness do not rest exclusively upon comprehension of physical surroundings. They recognize—finally—that in most high schools the American history course, foundation of the social studies program, for some reason does not have the quality it ought to possess. They see the apathy if not plain hostility of many secondary school students (and often their parents) toward American history.

Such sentiments are not peculiar to Indiana. Conversations with individuals from other parts of the country have persuaded the authors of this book that over the entire nation there is worry and doubt in regard to high school instruction in American history. After talking with people who have looked into schools in other states—such as Kentucky, where a governor's commission recently made an exhaustive study—the authors have concluded that Indiana schools are typical of those in most parts of the country, that the American history course faces the same problems in Indiana as in other states.

How can schools improve their course in American history? Some observers contend that the answer is better textbooks. They have a point. Many high school texts are catalogs of names and dates, thrown together in such drab prose that almost by design, it seems, they repel the bright, imaginative student. Other persons think that better audiovisual techniques might offer a solution. One sees evidence of this latter view in ever-increasing school budgets for films, film strips, recordings, maps, charts, and diagrams. A few people—very few—see television as the hope of the future. Television can help. In some schools it has assured a few minutes each day of solid instruction in history. Other school critics have seen salvation in revision of the social studies curriculum. In recent years many educators have devoted a great deal of attention to curriculum, and produced recommendations which they hope will "update" the social studies program.

Even so, the key factor in teaching American history, and for that matter any subject, is the teacher. The course will stand or fall according to his talent and energy. If he is informed, enthusiastic, imaginative, he does not need television, an array of audiovisual aids, or an unorthodox and presumably more sophisticated curriculum. He can offer a good course with any of the standard textbooks. Conversely, a reformed curriculum, spirited textbooks, and audiovisual aids cannot compensate for pedantry.

If the American history course falls short of desired quality, as the authors of this book believe, it follows, then, that the teacher must bear a large share of the responsibility.

Among school people and interested citizens who acknowledge the responsibility of teachers for weakness of the American history course, perhaps the most widely held view is that the athletic coach is the culprit. Coaches, poorly trained and uninterested in history but required by law to spend some time masquerading as teachers—so the theory goes—have overrun American history classrooms. The coach gravitates toward history because he and his superiors believe it is less complicated, requiring less training, than other so-called disciplines. The result is a course lacking in interest or imagination, resting on the pupil's ability to obtain knowledge furtively from the textbook amid the coach's ramblings about last Friday's game.

Another, more flattering view of the history teacher inspires equal loyalty with the above "devil" theory. It holds that with some unfortunate exceptions all other teachers of American history are dedicated individuals, grounded in history, burdened by poor curriculum and textbooks, struggling long hours at low pay to keep alive the American tradition.

If both sides of this analysis were accurate the task of updating the American history course would present few problems. But theory does not always comport with fact. No more than twenty per cent of American history students in Indiana are under charge of individuals whose first responsibility is coaching. The coach more often conducts classes in civics, driver training, health, and safety. Frequently he spends noncoaching time in guidance work. As for coaches in the American history classroom, not all of them lack intellect or intellectual curiosity. Occasional coach-teachers show unusual ability. Moreover, not all noncoaches who teach American history are informed, dedicated, or overworked. In terms of interest in history—reading of history, conversation about history, searching for historical interpretation—there seldom is much difference between the coach and noncoach.

What are other possible explanations for poor teaching in American history? One sometimes hears that American history attracts teachers of inferior ability, the dregs of the scholarly world who could not make the grade elsewhere. There is no way of measuring such a proposition. Intuition and impression readily concludes that in ability, initiative, and imagination the typical American history teacher is no worse—and no better— than the teacher of mathematics or literature, economics or chemistry. His intellectual horizons are about the same. He spends the same amount of time (practically none) keeping abreast of developments in his field. His course, like those of the rest of the teachers in the school, essentially is the textbook. His salary is less than that of the science or mathematics teacher, creating a morale problem of sorts, but most history teachers complain about salary discrimination and then labor on as best they can.

Trying to assess the teacher of American history, one should turn to college backgrounds. Here it is easy to strike fire. A great many American history teachers (45 per cent in Indiana) have bachelor's degrees in education. In addition to twenty or so credit hours of work in "professional education" courses, they have completed a "concentration area" in social studies, which usually includes a smattering of government, sociology, history, economics, geography, and anthropology. Boiled down, this sometimes means that the teacher of American history has completed no more than fifteen to eighteen hours of undergraduate work in history, a third or more of which probably has been in European history. It is not unusual for schools to dispatch teachers into the classroom with eight to twelve hours of college work in American history. Since much of the prospective teacher's work in history came in freshman-sophomore level survey courses, this means that he has had little exposure to historical literature, has only a faint idea of historical method and philosophy, has come into contact with historical interpretations that probably were dated (college textbooks have the same propensity as high school texts to be a decade or two behind the latest scholarship). A teacher who invades the classroom with such a background is akin to the soldier entering battle with a popgun.

True, according to the figures reported in Chapter 7 (whose reliability the authors question) half or more of Indiana's American history teachers completed enough work for an undergraduate major in history. But again, much of the work was in freshman-sophomore surveys, much of it in areas outside United States history.

American history teachers generally recognize the

poverty of their undergraduate training. In scores of interviews by the authors, teachers spoke regretfully of failure or inability during college days to take more work in history. A large majority considered what courses they did take in history and such related fields as government and economics, sociology and literature, as the most beneficial part of their college preparation for teaching. A large majority urged revision of the curriculum of teacher preparatory programs to allow far more work in the "subject area." Since historians were conducting these interviews, of course, teachers may have found it tempting to overstate the case and excuse their own shortcomings. Yet one could not avoid noting the near unanimity of opinion and the conviction with which most teachers expressed themselves on these points.

What about courses in education which formed a fair-sized part of teacher preparation? Again, teachers expressed strikingly similar views. They criticized much of the work required of them in education, contending that education courses were repetitious and lacking in substance, not realistic, stressing method rather than knowledge. Comment paralleled the findings in James D. Koerner's recent book, *The Miseducation of American Teachers*. Most teachers interviewed by the authors —like those talked to by Koerner—had a few kind words for their course in methods of teaching social studies. Some saw benefit in the course in educational psychology. The only spark of enthusiasm appeared when they

spoke of practice teaching—for most teachers a reward-
ing experience. A typical comment came from a teacher
who, referring to her courses in education, said: "I
thought they were rather worthless, except for practice
teaching. I got an awful lot out of that."

Teachers who lament undergraduate inadequacies
have excellent opportunity to initiate corrective action
in graduate school; most teachers eventually receive
master's degrees. Indiana state law requires such a degree within ten years after a teacher begins teaching.
Unfortunately, here is opportunity for professional advance which teachers of American history often do not
seize (although new licensing requirements in Indiana
may compel them to do so in the future). The master's
program of the history teacher usually seeks the M.S.
in Education degree, often a thirty-six-hour goulash of
courses ranging from driver education and guidance to
curricular integration of audiovisual media. Transcript
after transcript examined in connection with Indiana
University's Lilly fellowships in American history—ap-
plications from teachers usually a cut above average in
ability and interest in history—disclosed not a single
graduate course in history or a related subject.

There are several explanations for this failure to
study history in graduate school, and none reflects credit
upon the teacher of history. Education courses, taken at
a state university or a small college, are less difficult and
consume less time than courses in history at the same
institution; teachers have the natural ambition to

achieve maximum results with minimum energy. Then there often is just as much recognition for one course of study as for another: in the view of many high school administrators the M.S. in Education carries as much weight as the M.A. or M.A.T. in history. Some administrators place higher value on the education degree for classroom teachers. So why should the teacher seeking an advanced degree take the more tortuous path?

Teachers also choose the master's degree in education because of difficulty in securing admission to a subject-matter graduate program. Admission to candidacy for the M.A. in history at Indiana University requires virtually an undergraduate history major (twenty-five semester hours). Applicants for the M.A.T. program must show eighteen hours of history. Graduate students of history at Indiana must have an undergraduate average in history of B, or show excellent promise of doing B work as a graduate student. Many high school teachers do not have the requisite hours in history. Far more cannot meet the requirement of a B average or B potential, for the plain truth is (as any college of education dean will readily concede) that a large percentage of today's secondary school teachers were C students in undergraduate days and have done nothing since graduation to indicate improved performance in a tough graduate program. For many teachers there is no alternative to the graduate program in a school of education where admission standards are low. This is no criticism of schools of education. It might possibly be a criticism of academic departments which have failed to meet the needs of the typical classroom teacher by offering a graduate program for the average teacher.*

Some teachers go into graduate programs in education in search of a principal's license. Since the monetary rewards for good teaching seldom match those for administration, many teachers from the day they pass through the school portals for their first job have visions of sitting in the principal's office—complete with upholstered chair, intercom, and private secretary in the outer office. When working for a graduate degree they choose courses which count for a principal's license. Indiana law which requires the master's degree within ten years is not particular; the classroom teacher meets the law just as effectively by completing courses in school administration as courses in colonial history or twentieth-century American literature.

Finally, many teachers take graduate degrees in education rather than history (and no doubt, English, chemistry, and mathematics) because they can earn most of the credits for the degree within a few miles of home. Indiana University at Bloomington has regional campuses scattered over the state, and the Graduate Division of the School of Education has shown far more initiative than academic departments of the university in meeting the graduate-course needs of extension students. Each semester, at each of the regional

* At Indiana University some history teachers pursue an M.A.T. in social studies, but this program also requires a B potential.

campuses, the School of Education offers two to eight courses carrying graduate credit. It schedules different courses each year, thus obviating expensive summer sojourns on the Bloomington campus. The School of Education's extension program enables teachers to receive as many as eight or ten hours of graduate credit in the regular school year.

As for history offerings at Indiana University's regional campuses, they are sparse by comparison. Several of the regional campuses offer no history courses carrying graduate credit. And no regional campus offers more than two graduate history courses, usually given year after year by the same instructor. The history teacher wishing to do most of his graduate work at a regional campus near his home has no alternative to the M.S. in Education.

For assorted reasons, including budget and the extreme difficulty of staffing regional campuses with graduate instructors in "content" subjects, education offerings at the regional campuses will continue to be a powerful magnet drawing teachers to the M.S. in Education degree. But in the summer session of 1963 Indiana University's department of history introduced many teachers to a new history course carrying graduate credit, a home reading course in the history of the United States in the twentieth century. From a list of fifteen paperbacked volumes—including Henry F. Pringle's *Theodore Roosevelt,* Arthur S. Link's *Woodrow Wilson and the Progressive Era,* Frederick Lewis

Allen's *Only Yesterday* and *Since Yesterday,* John Kenneth Galbraith's *The Great Crash, 1929,* and Eric F. Goldman's *The Crucial Decade—and After—*each student selected twelve titles. After reading each book he prepared a thousand-word critical review. During the summer members of the department conferred with each student. As for the admission problem, the student could enroll in the course if he had secured admission as a transient student in the Graduate School, a regular student in the Graduate School, or a student in the Graduate Division of the School of Education. Publicity for this course did not reach teachers until the end of April, yet within the next month some three hundred teachers expressed interest. Many explained that commitments prevented them from enrolling in the 1963 summer session, but that they would welcome such a course during the regular school year or a subsequent summer. In the end eighty-two teachers enrolled, including a surprising number of elementary teachers. Results were gratifying. Critical reviews showed steady and in some cases remarkable improvement. Students showed rare enthusiasm, many of them conceding that this was their first concentrated reading effort since college.

Possibilities for courses of this kind are almost limitless. A history department could offer home reading courses with paperbacked volumes in ancient history, English history, Russian history, colonial America, the Civil War, the Negro in America, the French Revolution. Yet at this writing the future of the reading course is in doubt. With excellent reason university administrators look with some suspicion upon reading courses. How can a department insure standards? Will such a program deter students from coming to the campus for lecture-discussion courses and seminars which the university considers far superior to home reading courses? Then the course presents problems for a department of history. Is a professor's time well spent in a course such as this? What limit should the department impose upon credit hours toward a degree which the student earns via home reading? Still, the course offers opportunity of reaching a large group of history teachers who otherwise would have slight chance or incentive to enroll in graduate history courses. It deserves serious attention of college and university officials and history departments everywhere.

The cogent argument against the home reading course for graduate credit is that the high school history teacher should read books such as those by Pringle, Allen, and Goldman during spare time. The truth is that the typical teacher reads virtually nothing in his field from year to year. In the period of 1960–63 Indiana University historians in personal interviews asked hundreds of teachers of United States history: what have you read in American history during the past year? About eighty per cent of the teachers replied "nothing." Of the remaining twenty per cent about half had read something on the Civil War, usually a volume or two by that superb stylist Bruce Catton who has written extensively on the war's military campaigns. It seemed incredible to mention the names of prominent historians of the present day—Allan Nevins, Samuel Flagg Bemis, Lawrence H. Gipson, Samuel Eliot Morison—and draw a total blank from the history teacher. Most Hoosier teachers were not even familiar with the Bloomington department's renowned Pulitzer Prize-winner, R. Carlyle Buley.

Here, indeed, is much of the problem of the high school course in American history. Teachers rely on the fading memory of a few elementary college courses.

For outside visitors, observing high school classrooms is (as our college students would say) a traumatic experience. When the uninformed and nonreading teacher attempts to analyze or explain, the results are disastrous. In one classroom a student asked the teacher to explain the Monroe Doctrine. The teacher responded with an air of confidence and authority: "That was our attitude toward Europe plus Europe's attitude toward us." In another school a teacher explained that James K. Polk—who had been governor of Tennessee and speaker of the House of Representatives—was a political unknown before his presidential nomination in 1844. Another teacher announced that she hated to teach Grover Cleveland's presidency—the time of the Dawes Act, the Interstate Commerce Act, the Panic of 1893, the Populist revolt—because, she said, nothing happened.

Why does the teacher fail to read in the vast and exciting literature of American history? The usual explanation is lack of time. The teacher says that he has four or five classes each day. When he reaches home in the evening he is exhausted, yet has to grade papers and prepare the following day's classes. Four or five hours in the classroom can be strenuous, of course, although (as a subsequent chapter of this book will show) many teachers give upward of half of each classroom period to something educators euphoniously describe as "supervised study," during which the teacher usually meditates at his desk. As for preparing in the evenings, the classroom observer seldom sees much evidence. It takes little time to get up a list of questions from the textbook with which to interrogate students—standard operating procedure in American history courses. It takes little time to grade true-false and multiple-choice exams, s.o.p. in high schools. Such cynical appraisal, to be sure, is patently unfair to hard-working, imaginative, dedicated teachers of American history, but, the authors think, not to very many teachers. Finally, the teacher excusing his failure to read because of overwork in the classroom fails to note that there are only 180 school days per year. What does he do during the other 185? Few teachers are so burdened that they could not read history for fifteen minutes each day; this could result in reading ten or twelve books a year—ten or twelve more than some teachers read.

A more accurate explanation for this notable failure

to read, this failure to know books and historical interpretation, is that teachers come from an unbookish
background and teach in an unbookish environment.
College courses in education are not noted for stimulating great interest in reading. Neither are many college
courses in history, especially undergraduate courses
which often rest on dull lectures and dull textbooks.
When the teacher enters his high school he again en-
counters an unbookish atmosphere. The principal's
main concern is lunchrooms, teacher salaries, truancy,
the school board, unhappy parents; he seldom is a person of large intellectual interests. The school library
usually offers proof of these assertions; as a later chapter
will show, the typical high school library—which should
be a focal point of intellectual activity in the school—is
a little-used appendage or anachronism required by
law. (A recent meeting of librarians of Indiana and
Kentucky schools contradicted this appraisal, but the
authors have seen no reason to change their view.) The
young teacher quickly finds that other teachers do not
read books or dispatch students to the library. Around
the lunch table his colleagues never discuss historical
literature. One young teacher in a northern Indiana
school received ridicule from fellow history teachers for
spending spare moments reading.

One can offer endless illustrations of this unbookish
nonintellectual (as opposed to anti-intellectual) character of secondary school teachers. Recently, following a
new summer school course which Indiana University

set up for teachers ("Studies in American History for Teachers," emphasizing books and historical interpretation), a graduate student who during the regular school year taught history in a central Indiana secondary school said to his instructor approximately as follows: "You know, on the first day of summer school you casually mentioned such historians as Bemis, Commager, Nevins. I had no idea in the world who those people were." (This candid young man, now a candidate for a Ph.D in history, had exceptional intelligence, and was vegetating in his school—which was in a notable college town.)

To illustrate further, in 1960 two of the authors made up a short booklist in American history for high schools, had it mimeographed, and distributed it to teachers and librarians. Each of the 150 entries included author, title, publisher, and price. One librarian in a school of eight hundred students showed interest in the list (her neat and nicely furnished library had one book in American history, published in 1895). She ordered about forty titles. Six months later a check showed that the books made excellent appearance on the shelves, but not one had been taken out. Though informed about the purchases, the history teachers had not shown the slightest interest. Needless to say, the librarian had no inclination to pursue the matter further.

In another school the principal conceded that one of his American history teachers read little, but added that "I think he does a crackerjack of a job." Asked why the teacher did a good job, the principal replied: "He has good discipline. And that is one thing a principal looks at." In another conversation a teacher, asked if teachers in her school read books, replied: "I would say they resist it as much as possible." Later this same individual insisted that her school, staffed by these people who did not read, was a "prestige school."

Again, it is possible for teachers to read books on history. One Lilly fellow—during his first year of teaching (he had a wife and child) when he was preparing his history course from scratch, as well as a course in "safety"—read and reported on twenty-four books in recent American history, and in addition prepared a historical article which later appeared in a scholarly journal.

There are other aspects of the teacher problem. Many teachers unfortunately cannot concentrate upon their area of major interest. The trend toward consolidation of high schools may end this situation, but at the present time many history teachers have classes in government or economics or Spanish. They have to give some energy to these other areas. Then there is the matter of employment ouside the school. Not much "moonlighting" goes on during the regular school year (although one American history teacher worked after hours in a brewery), but many teachers, especially men, if they do not attend a college summer session, seek summer employment. During these twelve or so weeks the world of books and ideas provides few distractions for the teacher seeking to buy a bigger house or faster car. Professionally, of course, he is wasting his time.

Incidentally, an interesting way to solve the summer employment problem, so-called, would be for school boards to put teachers on eleven-month contracts, increasing teacher pay correspondingly over present contracts, and requiring such teachers to spend two summer months enrolled in subject-matter courses at the university, taken under an approved—by the university department of history—general plan of study. Such procedure would be far better than the present chaotic situation wherein teachers elect their own summer occupation, whether to drive a milk truck or study (and, if the latter, then to go off to an institute or some other smorgasbord of courses, often unrelated or without serious purpose, usually in the field of education rather than subject-matter). In the sciences, teacher training in the summer has recently received massive support from the Federal government, resulting in large numbers of institutes. But scientists in charge of these programs are becoming increasingly worried that the institutes provide no real leverage to ensure work by the teachers who often just "sit there" and wait for their scholarship checks. The institutes fail to "build a fire under" the teachers. There is talk in the sciences of persuading individual systems to put teachers on eleven-month contracts and force a regular program of advanced study. The same sort of thing ought to work in the social studies, particularly American history. Regular summer study programs for teachers would have the further advantage of making serious use of college campuses across the country, many of which lie embarrassingly idle—or are the scene of all sorts of embarrassingly pseudoacademic sideshows—during the summer.*

In looking at the teacher problem, there arises one final interesting point, namely, the amazing lack of *esprit de corps* among high school teachers of history. Seldom do they think of themselves as members of the historical "tribe"—and major responsibility here rests perhaps with college history departments and professional historical organizations which until recently have almost ignored the high school teacher and his problems. High school teachers look upon themselves as teachers who happen to teach history. They, therefore, associate good teaching with classroom technique rather than knowledge of history. A veteran teacher with thirty years of experience said recently that "study of history must always remain secondary to my teaching of history." The authors have seen this attitude in conversation with teachers eager to talk about new audiovisual aids and teacher handbooks, never about Arthur S. Link's ideas on Woodrow Wilson or John Hope Franklin's interpretation of Reconstruction. Few of them read any historical journal. The one national journal in American history, the well-known *Mississippi Valley Historical Review*, recently renamed *The*

* All university teachers afraid of the trimester system, for which there is a good deal of agitation, should support this sensible arrangement.

Journal of American History (edited, we add with pride, by members of the department of history of Indiana University) , draws as many blanks when put to history teachers as does the name of Allan Nevins. W. Stull Holt, who recently served as executive secretary of the American Historical Association, has remarked pointedly that "the number of high school teachers of history who have joined the major national organization of the historical profession is pitifully small. No exact statement is possible but the member of the staff of the American Historical Association who works most closely with its membership records estimates that the number of high school teachers may be as low as 300. That only this handful out of the 65 to 75,000 high school teachers of history and the social studies should have felt sufficiently identified with the historical profession to join its national body is a startling fact." And it goes without saying that history teachers, despite abundant opportunity in their home towns and counties, never dream of engaging in historical research and writing.

In conclusion, among the thirteen hundred or so persons holding forth in American history classrooms in Indiana there are many—perhaps fifteen or twenty per cent of the total—who read books, take interest in historical interpretation, understand the nature and use of history, range far beyond the textbook in their classrooms. But a figure of fifteen or twenty per cent is not satisfactory. Students deserve better odds.

2 | THE STUDENT

Any evaluation of the American history course, and evaluation of secondary education generally, must look at the student. It is he for whom the teacher, course, library, administration, and school exist. If from his training the student emerges with an informed and inquiring intellect, then the high school comes off well. If he does not possess some of the equipment for challenging his future (and this equipment includes knowledge of the American past), something is wrong.

Who can measure the student's learning, and how? There is no precise way to gauge high school training. Schools vary widely. Moreover, students can pass through the same school, take the same courses, study under the same teachers, and come out with greatly different results. Still, it is not impossible to get some idea about the training of students graduating from high schools. If year after year an observer comes in close contact with recent high school graduates from a state or region, he can get impressions about secondary education which he may not arbitrarily dismiss. Such an observer is the college instructor. Among college faculty members probably no one has better opportunity to evaluate high school training than the instructor in the American history survey course, which draws hundreds of freshmen each semester. Over a few years the survey instructor sees literally thousands of the brighter products of the high schools, the "cream of the crop," less than a year—often in three months—after high school graduation.

The survey course instructor will discover that his new students have little knowledge of American history. He may try to teach his college course on a sophisticated level, for he should be able to assume that his entering students have at least a skeletal knowledge of American history. After all, they have taken American history three times before arriving at college—in elementary school (fifth grade), junior high (eighth), and senior high (eleventh). But any history instructor who assumes much student knowledge will learn better. The plain truth is that the freshman in college—if one accepts the verdict of virtually every individual who attempts to teach college survey courses —has the scantiest knowledge of American history. He knows that Columbus discovered America, that the Pilgrims landed at Plymouth Rock, that George Washington was the hero of the American Revolution and first president of the Republic, that Abraham Lincoln freed the slaves. He has no idea about intellectual currents of early America, such as Puritanism and the Enlightment. He is ignorant of British colonial policy, mercantilism, social and economic trends in early America. Seldom can he explain a single tenet of Jeffersonian or Jacksonian Democracy (except to say that the latter exalted the spoils system), identify John Marshall, or explain the Missouri Compromise.

As for American history after the Civil War, the college freshman knows even less. Reflecting the distaste of his previous teachers for such subjects, he knows practically nothing about the growth of industry (other than having heard of John D. Rockefeller and Andrew Carnegie) or the growth of cities, perhaps the two principal changes in American life over the past century. He has not the vaguest notion about Social Darwinism and pragmatism, cannot identify Herbert Spencer or William James, cannot explain "free and unlimited coinage of silver at sixteen-to-one" (much less tell why people once became excited about it), cannot recall having heard of a Treaty of Washington (1871 or 1922, it does not matter), the National Recovery Administration, or the Platt Amendment. He cannot list the presidents since 1865, a surprise since the high school teacher often emphasizes national politics. Proof of this fact came recently when an instructor asked students in an American history survey course to name the post-Civil War presidents and give dates of their terms. One student had Herbert Hoover as president from 1949 to 1953, another had Woodrow Wilson president in the years 1941–45, another gave Franklin Roosevelt's term as 1901–05. Students listed Franklin Pierce, John Tyler, and James K. Polk as presidents after the Civil War. One student put down William McKinley as president from "1865 to 1900— until he was shot." No student had an accurate list.

The freshman student can produce other fascinating information. The same instructor gave students in American history survey courses a "map quiz." Fewer than ten per cent handled this juvenile examination without error. Students could not locate the Mississippi River, the principal mountain ranges, major cities, or even states. Texas became California, Minnesota became Illinois, Kentucky turned into Florida.

There is abundant evidence of recent high school graduates' ignorance of history. One young man went through high school with a nearly perfect record in history, his favorite subject. At the university he saw a poster advertising a lecture by a prominent scholar on the Compromise of 1850. Try as he might, he could not recall the Compromise—hardly a minor event in American history.

Then there were the "advanced credit" examinations at Indiana University in September 1963. Incoming freshmen who thought they might know enough American history to pass the equivalent of a two-hour final examination for one or both of the United States history survey courses (or the history of Western Civilization, American government, and others) could take an advanced credit test. Students receiving an A grade on an examination—for example, the three-credit-hour survey course in American history to 1865—would receive three credits and an A. Students receiving a B would have the option of taking three credits and a B, or could enroll in the course and work for a higher grade. Students receiving a C could receive "placement" (no grade, no credits)—that is, could thereby meet "field" or "concentration group" requirements (thus permitting more electives).

In arranging advanced credit examinations the department of history after some soul-searching went to great lengths to be generous. The examinations required no knowledge of historical literature or conflicting historical interpretation (in view of the failure of high school courses to emphasize books and interpretation, such material probably would have doomed every student signing for the examination). The exams merely required the kind of information ordinarily available in American history textbooks. Moreover, despite some faculty objection, students had the option of writing on any four out of eight listed essay topics, a larger option than students in regular courses receive.

There was no attempt to couch examinations in deceptive or obscure terms. One exam asked students to write four essays from the following topics: (1) reasons for discovery and settlement of the New World; (2) the "great migration" from England to North America in the seventeenth century; (3) a comparison of French and British colonies in America; (4) why the American colonies declared independence in 1776; (5) the origins and growth of political parties in the United States from 1790 to 1860; (6) Anglo-American relations from 1790 to 1865, or American relations with Spanish-speaking peoples from 1787 to 1850; (7) the influence of slavery upon American politics from 1787 to 1850, or slavery as a cause of the Civil War; (8) why the North won the Civil War. Another exam (for American history since 1865) asked students to write four essays from the following topics: (1) Reconstruction after the Civil War; (2) factors which made the United States the world's leader in industry; (3) causes and consequences of the Spanish-American War; (4) the Wilson administration's policy toward European belligerents in 1914–17; (5) aims, programs, and achievements of the New Deal; (6) an evaluation of Harry S. Truman as president; (7) America's contribution to Allied victory in 1917–18; (8) American military strategy and campaigns in 1941–45.

Results of advanced credit examinations did not cast much credit upon precollege training in American history. A total of 329 students attempted the exam in history to the year 1865. Not a single student received an A. There were seven B's and sixteen C's. Figures were slightly better for history since 1865. Fewer students, 132, attempted the examination. It was clear that many freshmen, having already taken the first exam, suddenly had recognized their deficiencies and forwent the second. For the latter there was one A, nine B's, eighteen C's.

Faculty members who graded the exams reported that the great majority were so poor (often fewer than three or four pages in an examination bluebook) that it was difficult to avoid giving excessive credit if students demonstrated any knowledge at all. In considering developments making possible the discovery and settlement of the New World, even the better informed students could not cite much beyond the compass and astrolabe, usually failing to note the intellectual ferment in Europe, appearance of nation states, improvements in ship construction and weapons, need for better trade routes to the East. Essays on the Declaration of Independence usually set out the old Fourth of July clichés. Students who attempted the essay on President Truman apparently had never heard of Potsdam, the Truman Doctrine, Marshall Plan, Berlin airlift, NATO, Point Four, or civil rights, remembering only that Truman ordered dropping of the atomic bomb and intervention in Korea. Equally interesting was the manner in which students shunned certain topics—such as President Wilson's policy toward Europe's belligerents in 1914–17, or the New Deal, two of the most important and frequently discussed topics of recent American history.

Bearing out the poor quality of precollege training is also the rate of failure of college freshmen in survey courses in American history—courses, one must recall, which presumably repeat much of what the student has learned several times before coming to college. It is not unusual for a fourth to a third of freshmen in such courses to receive grades of D or F.

Because the freshman student lacks knowledge, the survey courses in American history in college often become virtual high school courses, the instructor trying to get across information which the student theoretically had when he arrived on campus. If there were any correlation between theory and fact regarding the freshman's understanding of American history, it would be possible for most students to sidestep the survey courses and move immediately into advanced work in history. Here is the dream of history departments in most colleges and universities. But until the high schools start turning out students of much higher quality—at least students better grounded in American history—this dream has no chance of coming true.

Perhaps the inadequacies of the typical high school student of American history come from inability to read. Whether "Johnny can read" has received national attention in recent years. Many teachers—often poorer ones—complain that their students cannot read well, that they cannot understand the simplest textbook, let alone such a book as Walter Lord's uncomplicated eyewitness account of the Pearl Harbor attack, *Day of Infamy*. Although it is true that some high school students have serious reading problems, one often suspects that teachers exaggerate deficiencies to excuse a failure to require more reading and failure to present a course which is more than the textbook. For there are high school teachers who insist that students can read, and prove it by having them read books and prepare analytical reports and term papers. Classroom visits by the authors of the present book have found no large reading deficiencies of high school students. In a couple of classrooms the students read the textbook aloud, each student reading a few sentences or a paragraph. There was no stumbling. Occasionally such round-robin exercises brought forth questions, indicating comprehension.

The second fundamental skill is writing. Here again the college instructor has unique opportunity to measure high school training. The experience almost always is that freshman students have difficulty expressing themselves on paper. With practice—an essay examination or two, a few book reviews and term papers—performance improves remarkably, leading to the conclusion that high school students do not receive enough practice to learn good writing. A great many freshmen history students have reported, often with bitterness, that before coming to college they had never written an essay examination or term paper.

As for intellectual capacity, there is no reason to believe that the typical high school student cannot learn basic historical data and thereby arrive at historical generalizations. The high school student is not inept. But he probably will not acquire knowledge of history if no one is pushing him toward his capacity. One often hears that it is psychologically dangerous to apply undue pressure upon young minds for scholastic achievement. The critical word here is "undue." Too much is —to indulge a bright remark—too much. But there is no danger of psychic damage in the average high school. Interestingly, most history teachers admit that they do not try to get maximum effort from their students. The ordinary high school student, one soon discovers, moves along at an intellectual crawl.

All the foregoing about reading, writing, and intellectual capacity is not to argue that there are no differences in student ability, or that the teacher should ignore them. Ranges are wide, much wider than the college instructor must face. If the teacher aims a course at the bright students he frustrates the poor ones. If he lowers his sights he gets the opposite result. Most teachers shoot for the middle, a weak compromise. Ability-grouped courses present a possible solution to this problem. Many schools are running grouped courses with some success.

There are certain objections to ability grouping, but these make little sense. One argument is financial; small schools cannot afford extra classrooms and teachers. School consolidation, now getting into high gear, may solve this difficulty. More frequently one hears that grouping endangers the emotional well-being of students excluded from the top sections. The authors retain no psychologist, but doubt whether the price of soothing the slower student's psyche is worth the cost to society. Is it fair to hold back the bright student? Does he not deserve every intellectual advantage? The slower student is going to discover limits sooner or later. Discovery will be less of a blow in high school than later—when he fails in college or goes broke in business. One suspects that the real psychic blow of failure to qualify for the top ability groups does not fall on students; by the time they reach high school they know who the "smart kids" are. The heaviest blow falls, of course, on parents. Then there is the idea that both bright and dull students gain an important social experience from exposure to one another in the history classroom. This argument would have greater merit if its proponents could demonstrate that teachers are clever enough to stimulate and gain maximum performance from all students in nongraded classes.

With good teaching, ability-grouped classes can produce startling and highly gratifying results. One of the most successful superior student classes in the authors' experience is in a medium-sized northern Indiana school led by a teacher who likes books. The class is not the conventional eleventh-grade American history course, but a special proseminar in recent United States history for talented seniors. Students do not even receive credit for the course. But the fifteen or so who enroll each year examine interesting historical problems—Reconstruction after the Civil War, intellectual currents, the rise of America to world power, Pearl Harbor. Through the year they read all or parts of thirty-five or forty books, mostly paperbacked volumes which they can buy. Student and parent reaction has been enthusiastic. Some parents have begun to read the books which their sons and daughters carry home.

In concern for the bright or superior student the teacher must not overlook the needs of slower ones. The slow learner must and will make a contribution to society. If he functions on a different level than his more gifted chum, knowledge of history likewise is important to him.

But how does one interest today's lethargic students? Here probably is a more important matter than interesting slow or bright students. Relating history to present-day affairs is one device for arousing interest, an entirely proper procedure so long as history does not get lost in the discussion—as usually happens. Another technique is to focus on glamorous or exciting moments and people of American history, especially, say, the Civil War. Three or four weeks often go to the Civil War—not to its causes and consequences, mind you, but military campaigns. The Civil War has become an obsession with untold teachers, in part perhaps because of the centennial observance. With enthusiastic approval of students, who would rather turn their thoughts to Admiral Farragut damning torpedoes than the social philosophy of Lester Ward, teachers exhibit rifles and banners and uniforms and cannon balls and heaven knows what else. Elaborate maps show the mistakes of poor General Lew Wallace at Shiloh and poor General George Pickett at Gettysburg. Even so, the business of interesting today's lethargic student is difficult. It may be virtually impossible. Apart from and despite the most skillful teacher pyrotechnics, the most stimulating classroom discussion, despite the most beguiling historical topics and historical prose, the high school student has so many things to do, other than study.

One turns thus to student distractions. There should be some sympathy for the long-suffering history teacher trying to arouse interest in the American past. The most persistent distraction is the interscholastic athletic contest, one or two of which take place nearly every week of the school year. In many schools the principal dutifully eliminates a Friday class or two to permit students to attend pep rallies. Athletic enthusiasm in Indiana—known proudly as "Hoosier hysteria"—reaches a peak during a one-month period beginning in late February when the Indiana High School Athletic Association stages the State Basketball Tournament. During those

weeks Admiral Rickover would receive the most vehe-
ment abuse of his career if he came to Indiana for one
of his lectures urging abolition of all extracurricular
school activities.

The disturbing aspect of high school athletic enthusiasm is that students generally do not realize that recognition on the basketball court is short-lived, that towns
across the country are full of yesterday's sports heroes,
now forgotten. Students ignore admonitions that classroom success or failure can leave a permanent mark.
Much of the difficulty here rests with parents and towns-
people. In the last analysis it is the parent, merchant,
plumber, doctor, barber whose juvenile enthusiasm pro-
duces this ridiculous hysteria. In an Indiana township
recently the trustee courageously fired the basketball
coach whose teams had won a large percentage of their
games over a period of years. The coach's salary was
much larger than those of ordinary teachers, so the
trustee determined to get a lower-priced coach and
raise teacher salaries. For a time the trustee thought he
might be "run out of town on a rail."

In the category of serious student distractions there
also is employment, often for the purpose of buying
and maintaining an automobile. The authors, their
high school experience some years behind them, have
been amazed to hear teacher after teacher lament student "moonlighting." For many a student, teachers
report, a car becomes all-important, and he will labor
afternoon and evening to keep it running. During school

hours such a student marks time until the final bell, his thoughts on four-barrel carburetors, racing camshafts, and high-speed rear ends.

There are other distractions such as school plays, yearbooks, proms, things not bad in themselves but which in schools often assume positions of great importance and are time-consuming.

For many reasons, therefore, extracurricular and curricular, the typical high school student of American history puts little into and gets little out of his course. He spends a year on the course and then gladly turns to other things. He has no clear idea why he is taking American history, other than that law requires it. He rarely sees the course as a means to draw on the experience of his countrymen through many generations, to help him meet and understand current and future problems, to give greater understanding of the American character, Western civilization, mankind. He is not aware of the truth of the inscription on the statue on the Pennsylvania Avenue side of the National Archives building in Washington, which says that "The Past is Prologue." He does not know that the publisher Joseph Pulitzer listed knowledge of history as the first requisite for an editorial writer on a Pulitzer newspaper; Pulitzer thought that a reporter could not reach sound judgments about current affairs without understanding historic origins and the way in which people of the past coped with similar problems. For a great many high school students history is anachronism. Deep down, like Henry Ford, they think it is bunk.

3 | THE COURSE

In most high schools the United States history course is a chronological survey from the colonial beginnings to the twentieth century. Commencing in September with the era of discovery, the class proceeds through the centuries and normally arrives at the 1920's, or a bit later if all goes well, when the school term closes the following spring. In this span of over four hundred years, some topics attract more attention than others. Teachers and students have their favorite stations along the way, largely the same ones for all classes, and these points receive decidedly the heaviest emphasis. Typically, they are the period of exploration and colonization, the Indians, the Revolution, the Constitutional

Convention, the West, Andrew Jackson, the Civil War, and Theodore Roosevelt.

It is a rare and resolute teacher who manages to reach the post-1945 atomic age or even the presidency of Franklin D. Roosevelt. At the end of the spring semester only a few days are left for a hurried rush through the years beyond the First World War. A great many students have had the same experience in the junior high, and far too many will have it again if they enroll in a college introductory course. As a result they have no more than a casual acquaintance with the events and problems of the Great Depression, the New Deal, the Second World War, and the Cold War. Thus Hitler, Stalin, Hull, Bradley, MacArthur, and McCarthy may be names less familiar than Bradford, the Iroquois, Cornwallis, Clark, Boone, Calhoun, Lee, and the first Rockefeller.

Invariably there is a strong institutional accent. Limited to charters, constitutions, laws, elections, battles, courageous personal exploits, government reforms, and treaties, the usual course is basically a selected political history. Within these confines the teacher may lead his class into a veritable maze of information, though he will find it much more difficult to stimulate thought about the meaning of the facts. One of the reasons for the difficulty is the narrow path the teacher travels. Seldom does he venture into the broad and somewhat forbidding social, economic, and intellectual areas of history; and when he does, his transit is rapid.

Despite all the talk about the "new history" during the last half century, little of it has filtered into the classroom. Few courses push beyond the traditional horizons to explore the character of the people, industrial conditions, social patterns, or literature and ideas, all worth knowing by themselves and even more valuable when related to political movements and issues.

A problem causing widespread concern is the repetition of large parts of the subject as taught in the junior high when the student returns to them three years hence. Why do we have to found the colonies again and why do we have to refight the Civil War? These are familiar complaints. The sixteen-year-old may respond to the warmed-over facts by indifference or perhaps resentment. This is the third turn around (after the fifth and eighth grades), and those going on to college may expect still another voyage over the same route. Nothing is more likely to kill enthusiasm for history than to rattle the old bones time after time. And it is a disturbing fact that innumerable students come out of, if they do not go into, the course with a poor opinion of United States history. Today mathematics and science, not history, are arousing the youngsters' greatest interest.

To remedy some of these defects curriculum reformers have come forward with suggestions for improvement. Since the present eleventh-grade course has simply too much ground to cover, it is said, the thing to do is to divide all American history into two parts. Let the eighth-grade teacher begin with colonization and come up to the Civil War, and then take the story from there in the senior high (with a quick review of the preceding highlights) so that the class will have sufficient time to study the twentieth century. Many also propose abandoning or de-emphasizing the customary chronological treatment and introducing a topical approach. For example, they would study labor, foreign policy, and the status of the Negro as units all the way from 1865 to the present. Another plan currently gathering support would move the senior-high course down to the ninth grade and divide it with the eighth to make a two-year, integrated sequence. This would not only place the course in a logical curricular pattern, it is asserted, but would also provide a greater opportunity for the later study of European and non-Western history and other social sciences. Any one of the plans for dividing the course between the junior and senior high schools, contend the reformers, would have the virtues of eliminating needless, boring repetition and of helping to restore history to its rightful standing.

Though there are some credible arguments for the changes proposed, the inherent disadvantages are substantial. Foremost among them is the vast psychological gap between eighth-grade and eleventh-grade students. A child of thirteen does not have the same background of experience, the depth of understanding, and the maturity of judgment that he will have when he becomes sixteen. All these are indispensable to an effective study of history at a level expected, if not always achieved, in the senior high. To say that the eighth grader can work through a mass of evidence and develop useful concepts equivalent to those attainable by the eleventh grader is to defy both common sense and widely accepted scientific findings. Those who declare that they can teach any concept of the social studies at any level are not talking about the kind of mental process that most historians believe essential to the study of history. For one thing, no one can *teach* concepts. What the student learns in a history course is dependent upon his capacity and skills that develop as he grows older. He, not his teacher, will formulate viable ideas that will endure after he leaves school. Notwithstanding the desirability of introducing the junior-high child to his country's past, it is highly unrealistic to believe that he can learn all that is essential to American history up to 1865 and that he need never bother with it again. Many of the important and absorbing books that he should read would be simply incomprehensible at this juncture. Besides, if the individual's interest is a significant condition for learning, and few would gainsay this, he would miss in the eighth grade the most appealing phase of the course, the recent period where he can see closer connections between his study and the contemporary scene.

All these objections are also relevant to the proposal for moving the eleventh-grade course down to the ninth grade. Moreover the subject now needing greater strength would become still more shallow. Memorization of facts without much interpretation, emphasis upon dramatic effect instead of challenging ideas, and use of books lacking penetration and sophistication would be the consequences. Furthermore many school systems would face immense problems of organization and coordination, despite the reformers' intentions to make the pattern tidier. Where the elementary or junior high schools break with the senior highs at the end of the eighth grade, two different teachers in different schools and in quite different circumstances would be responsible for the two halves of the course. One can easily imagine the confusion that would ensue. Even after the most strenuous efforts to achieve unity and continuity in the course as a whole, the outcome would be just the opposite.

Every indication is that most teachers unhesitatingly oppose shifting United States history down to the ninth grade or dividing it with the eighth, and they do so on the grounds previously mentioned. They readily acknowledge that large improvements must come, but they do not think these alterations would be improvements. What support there is for the proposals comes principally from administrators, curriculum specialists, and a sprinkling of college professors, but many of them have their doubts and reservations. On this issue the views of the teachers seem more sound than those of the experts.

It is not enough, however, to disparage these recommendations, unwise and impractical though they are. The defects in the present course are painfully apparent, and there is no time to waste before doing something about them. After visiting dozens of classrooms and after talking with several hundred teachers, the authors of the present volume would like to offer some recommendations. The recommendations are concrete rather than theoretical and do not imply immediate perfection everywhere. Yet they do promise progress in the typical course for the average student, since they derive from the experience of able teachers who have tested them in the classroom itself.

First, the course should remain in the eleventh grade, or perhaps move up to the twelfth. If the history of the United States is as vital to secondary education as Americans have always thought it is, the schools cannot afford to weaken the subject in any way. As one of the very few courses required of all students, it should occupy a place in the curriculum where it will have the best intellectual substance and deliver the most durable values. This place would obviously be near the close of the high school program when the student is sufficiently mature to handle some of the complex materials and ideas charactcristic of real history. Admittedly, those who unfortunately drop out of school as soon as they become sixteen miss the American history course at this level, but moving it back to the junior high penalizes all the others who do not drop out. Surely there are better means of handling the dropout problem.

Second, the course should continue to be a chronological survey from the colonial beginnings to the present day. To eliminate any large block of time would considerably damage the subject by throwing it out of proportion and making it less intelligible. Nevertheless, no historian would contend that all facts are equal and demand the same degree of attention. Any history course has to be a selection of all that happened in the past. So the teacher must emphasize certain topics and slight others less important to his goals. If he does this skillfully, he will avoid some common mistakes. Particularly he will allow enough room for the recent period. He will not devote a month to the Civil War and two days or less to the Second World War. One who has not taught will little appreciate how difficult this is, but it is possible if the teacher exercises some restraint and lays his plans carefully.

Third, the course must be much broader than it is. Instead of the narrow political narrative, limping along as it does in many schools through dry-crusted elections and battles, it should become a study of the American past in a genuine sense. Some topics virtually ignored in the traditional course but essential to a profitable treatment of the subject are: immigration, industrialization, finance, labor, civil liberties, transcendentalism, social reform, pragmatism, and military-civil relations.

Reading materials, high in quality and easily understood by the high school student, are plentiful. Though they are not entirely deficient on such points, textbooks do need liberal supplementation both to convey meaning and to sustain interest. If the teacher recognizes the importance of these transfusions, he will find ways to administer them, the first step being to read the books himself.

Fourth, the course urgently needs depth. In more schools than one would like to count, students think the history of the United States is identical with their textbooks. Too many never read any more than they find there on the Second Bank of the United States, the abolitionists, Andrew Carnegie, or the Progressives. Therefore, they erroneously suppose that if an assertion of fact is in the textbook, it is the gospel truth. They never comprehend the fascinating, controversial nature of the big questions of history, about which even learned scholars exploring the frontiers of knowledge disagree, questions that demand thought as well as memory. When the senior high school course plunges into history at this depth, it will not "repeat" all that the students learned in the eighth grade.

Fifth, new courses and special sections in American history would be especially beneficial. An elective senior seminar on selected topics, handled in depth, might follow the existing survey for those serious-minded and gifted students willing to work up to their maximum. Some schools have been doing just this quite success-

fully. Another stride forward would be the establish-
ment of an advanced-placement section, taught at the
same level as the college course and preparing students
to take an examination for college credit. The advanced-
placement program in American history has been ex-
ceedingly popular and effective throughout the nation.
To accomplish these things, however, the teacher must
improve his knowledge of the subject and must expand
his library's holdings in the field very extensively. The
benefits to the average students in regular classes would
be as great as to the superior ones, for they would
then also have better qualified teachers and stronger
libraries.

Thus it is clear that the character of the reading
program is an accurate indicator of the quality of instruction. By and large, the program is anemic or nonexistent. Day after day the usual class plods through
the text a few pages at a time, and this provides the
only basis for discussions and examinations. Until he
breaks this pattern, the teacher will preside over a
superficial, boresome course.

Still, an increasing number of teachers are asking
their students to read. Here the problems are what to
require and how to relate it to the subject as a whole.
Typically, at the end of each six-week period the students submit reports, chiefly summarizing the contents
of the books. Few have to criticize and evaluate what
the authors say, and even fewer receive adequate guidance for doing so. The old procedure of permitting

students to enter contracts to read certain amounts to earn grades seems to be falling into disuse, and this is probably good riddance. An occasional teacher will assign term papers, which can be quite valuable, but he finds it difficult to grade so many, perhaps a total of 150, in the time available. Individual oral reports too often turn out to be humdrum affairs that do not make sense to anybody, including the reporter. Whatever the system, reading is seldom integrated with classroom activity. Almost everyone looks upon it as "extra" or "outside" the basic course.

What measures should the teacher adopt? Obviously more students should read more or, in many cases, begin to read. Making the statement is, of course, easier than obtaining the desired results; but fundamentally it is a matter of the teacher knowing and talking about books. If he does not read and enjoy reading, his students may not. To a large extent, the reverse is also true; though, human nature being what it is, he will have to push as well as inspire his charges. He must coordinate the reading program with class discussion so that what the student learns in the text and in other books is all part of the same process, the study of history. If the teacher will order multiple copies of key volumes for the library or ask his students to purchase some of the inexpensive but very good paperbacks now and then, he can assign the same books to the whole class. Then there will be a foundation for discussion by a reasonably well-informed group. Naturally he will expect more from superior students either in individual instances or preferably in sections divided according to ability. He should also frame his examinations so that they cover material beyond the textbook as well as in it. Indeed he can find no better means to emphasize and integrate reading, for students will quickly see the advantages of relating it to the rest of their work.

In addition to some amount of reading, a course constructed with due regard for the progressive philosophy of education would inevitably include a good many projects and activities. These "learning experiences" would receive quite as much, if not more, attention than reading books. So the classic unit plan urged upon the beginning teacher leaves ample room for field trips, handicrafts, illustrations, bulletin boards, panel discussions, committee meetings, audiovisual instruction, and dramatic presentations. It is this phase of the school program that has aroused much of the recent controversy concerning the status of secondary education. Scorching attacks emanate periodically from the typewriters of college professors in academic disciplines on the ground that all this simply wastes energy and interferes with learning the subject.

The present writers have a great deal of sympathy for the position of the critics. But as far as American history in the high school is concerned, the situation is far different from the one pictured. Visits to classrooms selected at random demonstrate that most of the arguments revolve around an abstract question. The vast majority of teachers forget or reject what their professors of education taught them; they set up their courses the way several generations of their predecessors did. They may use the bulletin board for news clippings on current events, occasionally bring in a film strip, sometimes require student notebooks, and frequently assign individual oral reports; but otherwise they do very little with activities. The total effect does not resemble what one would expect to find if he took seriously the professional literature on planning a unit.

There is need for improving this facet of the course too. It would be not only dogmatic but unwise to reject all projects and activities out of hand. If the teacher uses them sparingly and intelligently, he will find them helpful, especially to stimulate the interest of some students. Unquestionably they must not be the central part of the work but only devices to assist the class in its main business of understanding the nation's past. In each case the teacher must ask himself if the project or activity will consume a reasonable amount of time, will not divert his students' attention from the intellectual goals of the course, but will bear a close relationship to the discussion, reading, and examinations. Applying standards such as these, the competent teacher does not need anyone to tell him what to do.

Panel discussions and committee projects, however, are particularly suspect. Though the members of a panel doubtless learn something in preparing their presentation and develop a communicative skill, the rest of the class will usually lose more than they gain. They will probably sit back and daydream while the panel talks and later may launch into a disjointed, ill-informed discussion (under the false labels of "critical thinking" and "problem solving"). Fundamentally the trouble lies in the hopeless assumptions that (1) those who have studied and thought about a matter can "share" their knowledge with others who have not done so and that (2) this latter group can think critically without preparation. Most objectionable is the idea of leaving the work to a panel or a committee, a plain disservice to the class as a whole.

A dismaying feature of the average course immediately noticeable to the observer is the absence of planning. Again a wide disparity exists between theory and practice. The prospective teacher learns how to draw up plans for the entire course, for individual units, and for each daily period. When he is out on the job, he religiously follows the textbook, normally selected by other people, and tells his students to read the next ten pages for tomorrow. He makes little or no effort to organize the course so that it will use his own qualifications in the best possible fashion and will build upon the circumstances peculiar to his school.

Curriculum specialists and supervisors have long been attempting to make improvements. In a number of school systems they have held conferences, worked with committees of teachers, consulted with scholars in the colleges, referred to a wide variety of publications, and drafted guides or outlines for United States history in the high school. Then they have distributed the plan to all the history teachers in the city, though usually without insisting that the instructor follow it down to the last line. As a matter of fact, most teachers do not use the plans. It is not because the substance or quality of the guide is necessarily defective, but rather because nearly everyone is reluctant to follow, or incapable of following, another person's plan. Obviously, teachers are abdicating their initiative to a far greater degree when they pursue the worn paths of textbook authors as faithfully as they do, yet to this they do not object.

Periodically there are renewed efforts to achieve uniformity and to intensify interest. Fresh proposals, more conferences, further expert advice, and revised guides follow, but very often with not much different results. The gap between the ideal and the practice remains wide. Recently in Indiana a committee appointed by the superintendent of public instruction labored long and hard to remodel the United States history course, as well as others in the social sciences, so that teachers everywhere in the state will have an instrument for resuscitating the subject. This is not the first, nor will it be the last, search for a formula of progress to pass on to the overburdened and undertrained teacher; yet at this moment it would be quite optimistic indeed to predict that the committee's recommendations will really take hold. To say this is not to deprecate what may be an attractive and sound structure for the course, but only to recognize the fate of previous attempts. The majority of teachers will probably not put it to work. Anybody's plan passed on to others seems destined to the same kind of ineffectual end.

The remedy, if there is one, consists in helping the individual to make his own plan instead of giving him one. By no means should one find fault with having plans, for their absence generally is a regrettable defect of the existing course. To avoid an aimless trail across the subject, to maintain the desirable pace during the school year, to introduce essential substance, and to adjust the course to the particular class, nothing is more important than the teacher's forethought. In the act of devising his own plan, he will have to think deeply about a good many topics. As he escapes the textbook prison, he will undoubtedly see why he must read more widely; and his students will too.

But how should the teacher proceed specifically? There is no single and final answer to such a question, though a few suggestions are appropriate. He will probably feel very keenly the superficiality of his preparation in the field and the limited opportunities, in terms of time and resources, to increase his familiarity with the subject. There is nothing wrong in considering the outlines of others or in relying upon some of the available shortcuts (such as the valuable pamphlet series published by the American Historical Association's Service Center for Teachers). Yet these can only be points of departure and not magic formulas to bypass the teacher's responsibility to study history himself. Furthermore whatever plan he adopts should not be fixed, but modified as a result of experience from year to year. Complacent adherence to a pattern over a long period will not maintain the same quality; it will certainly cause the quality to deteriorate. Another practice he should avoid is to schedule far in advance each detail down to the last day and minute. He will lose the flexibility he requires as unpredictable circumstances arise. And modern high schools being what they are, the harried teacher all too often finds that extracurricular activities, special assemblies, and pep rallies throw the best-laid plans into complete chaos. Here, by the way, he needs help—more than he is getting—from an academically minded, iron-willed principal. In short, the plan must be the teacher's own, it must improve with time, it must be flexible, and it must be attainable.

Any firsthand observation of the course in United States history uncovers numerous weaknesses. In the large majority of schools it is a narrow, shallow review of sacred political items, drawn almost exclusively from the textbook and failing to come closer to the present than a generation ago. One can sympathize with the motives of curriculum reformers who propose redistributing the course's contents between the junior and senior highs, for bold changes are necessary. But the changes they advocate are not desirable either psychologically or academically. The most promising path of progress is to improve the existing eleventh-grade chronological survey by making it broader and more penetrating. For this to occur, the teacher has much to do. He must know and use the literature of the field, he must involve his students in the absorbing intellectual process of historical study, and he must realistically plan each part of the subject so that it fits the situation of his own classroom.

4 | THE CLASSROOM

The scene is an American history classroom. The teacher is talking about the Great Depression of the 1930's.

Teacher: "The Great Depression was a most difficult time in the history of our country."

Students write hurriedly in notebooks, copying what the teacher has said.

"Many millions of people were out of work."

Busy writing in the notebooks.

"They had very little money."

Less writing in the notebooks.

"They didn't know where their next meal was coming from."

Practically no writing in the notebooks. Some students stare out the window to see who is playing football on the field outside. Most of the class surreptitiously begins to read the textbooks which lie open on their desks. They act as if they are studying material supplementary to the teacher's comments.

The teacher looks annoyed. He asks a question about the Great Depression.

The student named says nothing but looks startled, as if the teacher had been unfair.

Teacher asks another student.

Student stammers a wrong answer. Meanwhile his fellow students have paged their books furiously to find the right answer. Another student puts up his hand, and recites the correct answer.

The teacher looks relieved, and proceeds: "People were selling apples on the street corners. . . ."

It is about 11:07 and the clock, firmly in view at the front of the classroom, must move inexorably around to 11:55 before the commentary will end. Several students begin to dream of apples on street corners. Some students continue to look out the window at the physical education class. Sounds of a march come oomphing up from downstairs, as the school band practices. A door slams as a late student comes in, walks fearlessly to the teacher's desk and hands in a pink slip showing proper excuse, then proceeds down the aisle with snappy step to his seat.

The teacher is still elaborating on the Great Depression, and senses that the class has left him once more, either to do the next week's homework in the open textbooks (and thus avoid taking the books home) or to listen to the band or look out the window or watch the flies crawl around on the big glass globes under the lights. If the classroom is a new room there will be brightly colored maps on the wall, and student minds can chase up and down the coast of Africa or the Far East. There may be a chart showing the brightly colored insides of a human being. Or a poster left over from yesterday's election ("Be choosey, vote for Suzy," "Stick to Sue like glue").

The teacher moves slowly through the New Deal, the AAA, the WPA, and the PWA. He will ask a question, and a student will look up the answer in the textbook and give it back. So it goes, down to 11:55 and the bell.

It is like going through the Sahara, the Great Sahara of the intellect. The teacher is offering advice about the Great Depression, a few points he learned from his parents (the teacher was born in 1937). He is dispensing what he has looked up in his college textbook, perhaps a book by a man named Ricks or Hicks or Sticks (the book has a red cover and double-column print). He did this preliminary study last night, from 6:40 P.M. until a few minutes after 7:00, when he had

to go out. One should add that the class's textbook
which the teacher read two years ago is a boildown
of the book by Ricks-Hicks-Sticks, and it has everything
the teacher said in his talk.

Hence—and this is the point of the above photograph
of a class session in American history dealing with the
Great Depression—if one were to calculate the intellectual achievement of a 55-minute period conducted in
this manner there would be a very interesting result.
The teacher's remarks would have amounted to about
three or four pages of a college textbook. The students
because of distractions would have heard perhaps the
equivalent of two or three pages of the college textbook.
Meanwhile they were trying to catch up on the homework through furtive reading, of their own textbooks,
and indeed managed to read three or four pages. If
one compressed this intellectual activity into an intellectual result, it might have totaled a half-dozen pages
of textbook reading in nearly an hour. Considering
that a good student, even a fair one, should be able
to read three times that amount of textbook in an hour,
it is not difficult to see that this kind of work in school
is not effective. It surely would have saved the energy
of the teacher, and that of the students, if someone
could have decreed fifty-five minutes of silence during
which everyone could have read a good book. The
teacher might have read a good book, also, and turned it
into a properly prepared talk the next day—a talk on
material not in the class's textbook.

Perhaps, however, the teacher should not have talked. Many teachers believe that a high school student is too immature to follow a monologue, that he will become bored after a few minutes, perhaps ten or fifteen, and then the teacher's commentary should turn into a discussion.

This is a difficult point—whether virtual college-style lectures are effective. It does seem true that the average American today, adult as well as adolescent, has changed greatly from adults of two or three generations ago, so that it no longer is possible to hold a group's attention with a lecture unless the lecturer has extraordinary ability. The reason for the short span of attention by today's and tomorrow's citizens is difficult to ascertain. Perhaps the pace of life now is such that lectures no longer hold their onetime charm. In the nineteenth century a speaker could talk for hours and his audience listened with rapt attention, feeling that if the speech were only an hour or so long they had not received their money's worth. Daniel Webster and some of the other great orators could talk on for days. It is well known that Edward Everett in 1863 talked for two hours before the President of the United States made a few remarks in dedication of the military cemetery at Gettysburg, and that when Lincoln spoke only a few minutes—even if he gave the greatest address in the history of the United States, one of the great speeches of all time—his auditors went away disappointed. Those times are gone, and any Protestant clergyman of the present second half of the twentieth century who thinks he can take his sermons beyond ten or fifteen minutes will find himself brought up short by his parishioners. The span of popular attention appears short indeed.

It may be possible to conclude that long speeches and lectures in the nineteenth century were considered educational ventures, and people listened because they felt they were getting something which could not come easily otherwise. Now, surrounded by television and radio and telephone, the citizen finds himself under a barrage of words and will turn off his mind, if not his manners, if he has to listen more than ten or fifteen minutes.

Even so, lectures can be valuable in the average high school class in American history. Good lecturing is never easy. Many teachers also are not temperamentally suited to lecturing—they have no showmanship and sheer animal force. But if they have the temperament; and if they will keep the attention of the students, either by "pop quizzes" on the lectures or else by demanding, through strictest discipline, that students not dream and look out the window during a lecturer's time; and if they make serious preparation: the result can be highly beneficial.

Alternatives to lecturing are discussion or so-called supervised study. There is much public feeling that democratic training requires discussion among students, quite apart from any information derived from it. One

also might say that if discussion is of a fairly serious—
that is, informed—nature, wherein there is some pooling
of ideas leading to conclusions of merit, it has un-
doubted intellectual value. Discussion, moreover, is
fairly easy; it is not difficult to conduct a kind of dialogue
between students and teacher in which teacher asks
and students answer, especially under the present-day
habit of open textbooks on the desk. But it is possible
to consume hours in this kind of slow classroom col-
loquy. And to extract sensible talk from a group of
awkward high school students is no simple task; many
teachers who find lecturing difficult find discussion more
so. Much class discussion is utter waste of time. One
of the most disappointing aspects of high school classrooms in American history is the vacuity of the historical
discussion, the woodenness and irrelevance of the talk.
Many discussions are no more than clever efforts by
students (who might well devote their ingenuity to
something serious) to string out the class until the bell
rings.

One turns then to a method of teaching known as
supervised study. The first chapter of the present book
has touched upon it. Supporters of this method maintain that the teacher needs to give personal attention to
students, especially to guide student reading, and that
by turning a class loose on a textbook assignment during
class time the teacher can move up and down the rows
and deal with individual reading problems. This idea
has some merit, but directed study can turn into an

academic boondoggle on the part of both students and teachers. The students can look so convincingly alert, as everyone sits primly at the desks with book in hand; but the minds, if one could lift the tops from student heads and peer inside, often would be moving in convolutions entirely unrelated to American history. Discerning teachers know that students are capable of dreaming for long periods of time, and that what might seem to an adult as an impossible amount of time wasted is just an episode in a student's general intellectual nirvana. Many students do not yet have large interests in life; too many concerns of adults are to them only matters of theory; they have no thoughts of numbered years and sadly missed opportunities.

Supervised study may also be a refuge for the lazy teacher. High school teachers customarily look down their noses at the easy schedules of university teachers, remarking that the average college instructor might have only six or nine or twelve hours of classroom activity—lecturing—per week, whereas public school teachers average five hours of instruction a day, five days a week. But if one were to subtract a third of the public school periods, considering that many high school teachers spend one third of their time in class watching students read, it turns out that the high school teacher is doing not much more serious action in front of a class than his supposedly privileged brother in the university. And if one calculates the vacuity of so many of the discussions in high school classes, and the tautological nature of so many high school history lectures, the high school teacher may not have so difficult a task after all. For the poorer high school teacher the fashion of supervised study is a golden opportunity to "goof off." Many school systems have rules, or careful practices, that half of class time in such subjects as American history should be supervised study. Some teachers do not follow these rules or practices, but many do.

Almost all teachers, good or bad, whether for or against supervised study, agree that supervised study in individual classrooms is greatly preferable to study halls and that the latter should be abolished. There is absolutely no doubt that study halls, a hundred or more students in large cavernous places such as the cafeteria, auditorium, or even a gymnasium, are an ineffective intellectual practice. Study halls probably were an impossibility from the outset; a large group of young people confined to any space, even a well-designed study hall, find greater interest in each other than in their books. For good reason high school teachers of American history think study halls "a complete waste of time." The study hall teacher is a "keeper," like the officials at the zoo. He is a baby-sitter. Of course, study halls are administrative aids, giving a place for disposition of student bodies between different classes; they are of great help in scheduling, in both large and small schools. And study halls in the morning tend to be fairly effective, as some students have not yet done their homework and will be industrious. As the day passes the study halls get ever more riotous, until the nadir of a teacher's chores can come if he gets a study hall just before the end of school.

There are serious problems involved in abolishing study halls, and no amount of appeal to the intellectual value of such an act will suffice to answer all the arguments in favor of retention. It is clear that with the plethora of student automobiles in the average high school, and the manner in which various places of repute and ill repute—stores and restaurants and pool halls and bars, etc.—encircle the average city high school, there could be serious disciplinary breaches if students, with their skilled adolescent irresponsibility, were allowed to wander in and out of the school premises at will. No principal or superintendent could confront this situation with ease, and will tend to argue that it is better to have a little monkey business in the study halls than the simian activities that would follow from abolishing them.

But it does seem that the futility of study halls argues for their abolition. There is something intellectually frightening about the manner in which high school students almost call into question the use of knowledge, the importance of studying books, when they "cut up" in study hall. It is open defiance of the teachers and their supervisors, a gross affront to the entire school system. No outsider can watch a study hall long without a feeling of overwhelming anger.

The above discussion has raised, implicitly, the subject of homework, that concern of all teachers of the social studies, especially history which is a discipline best learned from books. The homework requirement for students in the average high school class in American history varies from nothing to perhaps a half or three quarters of an hour a night. Teachers have no clear idea of how much homework their students do. They always answer that "of course" the students are busy at homework, but discreet inquiry as to the amount and times of assignment and the manner in which teachers check to see that students do the reading shows that homework in many, many cases is a nominal accompaniment of the history classroom. The truth is that reading is often hard work, that even an adult will find a book boring or at least energy draining. There is great temptation not to read, even when the spirit is willing and when there is general understanding of the advantage of extending one's experience and fortifying judgment through the marvelous written word. Students often manage to back out of homework, sometimes with assistance of their teachers who are too interested in maintaining "student interest" (that is, teacher popularity).

Because today's youngsters have other courses and many extracurricular tasks is it unrealistic to expect high school students to study during evenings? There are many pursuits by the youth of today which are culturally or socially valuable—Boy Scouts or Girl Scouts, music practice, going to concerts, a welter of activities which make a better adult and which the requirements of formal education necessarily exclude from the classroom. Time has to be found for many of these activities, and no one can argue otherwise.

There is even contention that many high school students have jobs, and need release from homework to earn the money which, with good luck, will see them through a part or all of their college education. With tuition having risen to a thousand dollars or more at many private colleges and universities, with the high cost of dormitory life and the incidental costs of college, it is inevitable that the average family—facing an annual expenditure of from $1,500 to $3,000 a year with only one child in college—will see good reason for the child to earn part of his way.

The average family with children in high school has tended to accept the practice of individual school systems, believing that if a system does not assign much homework then this is the nature of present-day high school instruction, which is more efficient than in former times. Or else the family will believe that their children are brighter than normal and do not need homework which, undoubtedly, other students have to do.

Despite such misunderstanding, there must be more homework in such courses as high school American history where reading is so important. Many of the better students have band or some other school activity and have no study hall and therefore little school time to read. There is no use counting on supervised study in the classrooms, which even if effective would not be time enough. Teachers of the American history course are in a secure position for assigning more homework, as their course is required—students cannot, as they often do in college and the university, dash off to easier courses; the American history teacher has the key to an essential gate, through which all students have to pass, and he can and should extract a proper performance before passing them.

The argument that students need to work so they can save money to go to college often is a flimsy excuse to allow support of automobiles (half of all high school senior boys in the United States own an automobile). For girls a job permits purchase of extra clothing, or pin money for unnecessary trips. And anyway, if working were necessary for a student to go on to college, there is no reason to do it on the high school's homework time. Far better if the student with college financial problems worked a year or two between high school graduation and college entrance.

Assuming that the high schools need to tighten up on homework, one passes to the question of examinations. Here is that citadel of the teacher, the written confrontation between teacher and taught, proof of the pudding.

As every teacher knows, there is no single way to give an effective examination in American history. There are advantages to both essay and so-called factual tests.

Essays certainly are essential. Only through essays can the student gather the pieces of his information and make them meaningful; the essay will broaden a student's mind in a way that no other testing can; essays are utterly necessary "tools" to the high school teacher of American history. Probably the high school history essay should verge toward the disgorging of factual information, as the typical student in the course has not yet learned enough to deal altogether intelligently with ideas. It would be futile to expect highly intellectual answers to broad and general questions about the course of American national development; such essays will tempt the weaker students into clichés and the stronger students into facile expression of more complex clichés. Nonetheless, it should be a rule that no high school course is complete without frequent essays, written in clear prose, correct sentences, and proper paragraphs—topic sentences and all, with no irrelevancy.

A word to the teacher who has to grade such essays. Many teachers of American history have commented on the impossibility of essays in their courses—except at infrequent intervals—because of the time needed to read the examinations. It is not being flippant, debasing the coinage of teaching, to say that a good teacher does not read everything his students write. All college teachers of some experience know how it is possible to skim an essay, and this fact has not registered with many high school teachers. There is a fussy approach to essay grading which is entirely unnecessary. Perhaps the literalness comes from the high school tendency to give numerical grades—which are an invention of the Devil. No teacher can accurately tell the difference between 93 and 94, B plus and A minus. The sensible recourse is to grade essay examinations on the basis of alphabetical marks, without plus or minus perhaps, and thus facilitate skimming through the huge stacks of prose. The importance to student, as well as teacher, will be large, for with frequent essays and the impression—the facade is necessary here—that the teacher is reading them, the student will get a considerable prose experience and profit greatly thereby. At the same time, as mentioned, the teacher can have the best of both worlds.

How to give the needed impression of reading a skimmed essay? A mark here and there—a circled misspelling, an exclamation in the margin, a telltale check mark.

If one grades by alphabetical marks, without minus or plus, the categories come easily to mind. It takes little time to separate the extremes, the A and D and F grades. The only problem is the middle, B and C, which slightly more attention to those examinations will solve.*

* Few points in this volume elicited so much advance protest as the above argument about skimming essays. One of the book's authors (Maurice G. Baxter) heartily disagrees. A respected colleague at Indiana University (Charles Leonard Lundin) remarks that the whole notion is dishonest: "I disagree with this whole idea. If a student gets by with sloppy work, he has learned something wrong. What is

As for factual examinations, these will prove a necessary check on the teacher's essay-reading, and will have
other virtues. They enable the teacher to get into the
fine print of the assignments, necessary for prodding
laggard readers. They can cover a great deal of material,
as well as detail. They are easy to make up and grade.
Students in time-honored fashion will object that memory is no route to knowledge, and will cite the forget-rate
of factual information which may in truth be fairly
high. Students will find respectable intellectual reasons
why an American history course should not be taught
in so factual a fashion, and will not hesitate to embarrass
a teacher by implying that American history is "dead
as it can be," like the old rhyme some of us old-timers
learned about Latin. The good teacher will ignore this
adolescent scholasticism and move ahead through the
detailed factual examinations. *Per ardua ad astra.*

Three aspects of the classroom remain: current
events; audiovisual materials; television teaching. It is
only possible to touch on each.

The American history course is properly a place for
discussion of current events, and the only question is
how to do it. Certainly students struggling with the
relevancies of American history to the present may
abide the slower pace of the past if they can glimpse
the present-day tie-up. There has been a saddeningly

---

necessary is a lighter load for the teacher, so that he can do a more
thorough job. A single essay test in the course of the year, conscien-
tiously and helpfully graded, would be better than several with faked
grades."

large group of recent events susceptible of special explanation in the American history classroom. The Cuban
invasion failure of 1961 was worth talking about. The
confrontation over Cuba between Premier Nikita
Khrushchev and President John F. Kennedy in October
1962, the most dangerous world crisis since 1945,
was worth long explanation. The assassination of President Kennedy in November 1963 raised questions about
the entire history and future of the United States. But
how to introduce current events in the classroom. One
teacher had students read the *Wall Street Journal* and
the *Christian Science Monitor*. Another assigned a
student group to the *New Republic* and a second group
to the *National Review*. Most schools still buy a weekly
newspaper, in bulk or several copies—usually the
American Observer or *Senior Scholastic*. Sometimes
schools purchase bulk copies of *Time Magazine* or
Newsweek or *U. S. News,* or teachers assign reading
in them from the school library or subscription copies
at home. Often there then is a Friday panel discussion
on a topic of seeming student interest. The tendency,
however, is to cut down on current events, perhaps in
realization that the 1920's and 1930's spawned the
current-events idea, and that the hectic nuclear age
does not lend itself to sharing of classroom opinion and
casual reading. Events in today's world happen with
incredible speed. It may be that about all the teacher
can do is to point out the relevancies of the truly large
present developments to the past; and for the rest of it

stock the school library with daily newspapers and perhaps post a paper on the bulletin board and trust that by increasing knowledge of the past there will be increased desire to learn about the present.

The paraphernalia of audiovisual materials now available for teaching of American history—how should one use it? Audiovisual materials are generally low in intellectual quality and costly to purchase (both machinery and material) . They are tricky to set up, requiring an inordinate amount of teacher time. Film strips, juxtaposition of still pictures and text, have seemed silly and puerile, resulting in a good deal of student sleep in darkened rooms. Specially created movies have more point, but many of them are barely relevant to a serious American history course. Some newsreels are of high value, notably such a newsreel medley of the 1920's as the "Chronicle of America's Jazz Age," a film which showed commercially in the early 1950's. But after all the to-do of getting up audiovisual materials, equipping special rooms and acquiring film by purchase or borrowing by mail, after instruction of teachers in audiovisual techniques in graduate university courses offering two or three hours of course credit toward degrees—after all the hullaballoo one could probably erase the audiovisual activity from the American history course with no great loss and, in many individual cases, considerable gain.

One comes to television teaching. Here is a novelty in the educational world which attracts high schools,

giving opportunity to organize large classes and bring
first-rate lecturers to the students. Superficially considered (the reader can almost sense the drift of the
present analysis) television teaching does offer advantages. In Indiana the Midwest Program on Airborne
Television Instruction (MPATI) has been a pacemaker
for the nation. American history can come into most
of the state's schools by TV. Many schools have set
up receiving sets and organized classes.

This enterprise, though, has not proved itself. The
trouble is that organizing TV classes is a large business
which in complication may easily offset the benefits.
Many teachers are "down on" TV, because of both
hearsay and experience. They remark the expense of
TV receivers. There is difficulty in finding adequate
rooms in school buildings constructed when this sort
of teaching was beyond anticipation. Often the school
cafeteria has to take the receiving sets, and this means
a blending of dish-noise in the kitchen and the wonder-
ful smells of lunch cooking in the nearby vats. There
is trouble policing the large classes, to stop the inevitable
inattention on the part of at least a few students. Teachers are unsure of the progress of the TV lecturer, do
not quite know what he will cover from day to day.
The frequent changes of school hours for a pep rally
or some other activity mutilate or cut out telecasts.
There are days when the weather clouds over, and
the plane flying high above the Purdue campus cannot
send anything more than static and weird lines; local

teachers have to hold attention with impromptu lectures.

The prime complaint about TV teaching of American history concerns filling in time before and after the telecast—the ten-minute or fifteen-minute gaps before and after the telecast when the local teacher has to do something. To bridge these gaps the receiving teacher has to be an extremely clever person, probably much better than the average classroom teacher, for discussion is difficult with the large groups of a hundred or more students. There also is trouble in assigning homework and giving examinations over the disparate slices of telecast and local discussion.

The physical operation of the enterprise is formidable. The hope of some school systems that television teaching will cut down the number of classroom teachers has proved illusory. Any system which eliminates teachers as a result of TV teaching is almost certainly cutting the intellectual content of the course.

It may well appear as if the above commentary on the classroom is reactionary in the extreme, calling for more lectures bolstered by more quizzes and discipline and teacher preparation, for less discussion, for less supervised study, abolition of study halls, assignment of far more homework, both essay and factual tests, less current events, less audiovisual, perhaps less television teaching. It sounds like a desire to go back to the good old days of high school teaching, the antediluvian situation at the turn of the twentieth century when the high schools contained only potential college students. One must say in response that wasted time is wasted time, regardless of the IQ's of the time-wasters. That there has been something wrong with the average classroom in high school American history admits little doubt. So, since the prevailing technique has not been an overwhelming success, why not try some other—perhaps older—way?

5 | THE LIBRARY

One can learn much about a school's academic health by visiting its library. Looking at the shelves that hold the books in American history and flipping through the catalog cards give a quick impression of what materials the classes in that subject may be reading. An examination of the charge slips stamped with withdrawal dates provides an even better estimate of the character of the students' work. It is profitable also to browse in the reference, periodical, and newspaper sections to evaluate the resources available for reports and for term papers. Most librarians are willing to pause in their endlessly demanding routine to talk with the visitor about the library's role in the educational program, its past problems, and present prospects. And most revealing of all is merely to sit in the room for two or three periods and watch the students select their materials and use them for the next fifty or so minutes.

The visitor does not have to be an expert to detect at first glance a disturbing situation. With few exceptions the libraries are obviously deficient in sheer numbers of items. A medium-sized school having an enrollment of five hundred is likely to have a grand total of few hundred volumes, or less, touching American history. This would include not only sets, monographs, and biographies but relevant works in other fields such as political science and English (historical novels, for example). In old schools the backbone of the collection consists of books published in the early years of this century; in new schools, particularly many county or township consolidated institutions, the striking feature is the expanse of empty shelves. The library room in an old school, and some do not serve that purpose only, is typically small and badly overcrowded, so that the shortage of books is somewhat less apparent. The room in a newly constructed school is a complex of stainless steel, glass walls, comfortable seating arrangements, attractive appointments, modern lighting, but a very modest number of volumes on its pleasingly veneered shelves.

Still, the fundamental trouble lies in the quality

instead of the quantity of the holdings. There is an
oversupply of superficial, popular writings hardly de-
serving the label of history—fictional accounts written
down to a reading level below that of the students using
the library. Or there are dusty, ponderous tomes bound
to kill whatever incipient interest the young people may
have. Among the first group is an inordinate number
of biographies of sports figures; thus one may well find
several of Babe Ruth and none of Jefferson. Among
the second group are such works as the hoary *American
Statesmen Series* and nearly untouched sets of Schouler's
or Rhodes' histories, or others as dismal and less respectable. Between these extremes of shallow and
pedestrian literature is rather barren ground.

A further defect, even in moderately stocked libraries,
is a lack of balance in the collections. Political and
military narratives are dominant at the expense of
social, economic, and intellectual studies, a situation
reflecting the traditional shape of the course. The de-
tails of the election of 1876 might be easy to find, but
the character of Social Darwinism might not. A library
is unusual if it has the full set of the *History of American Life*; it is more so if it has any volume of the
Rinehart *Economic History of the United States*. As a
result, a student with enough intellectual curiosity to
go beyond the tight limits of his textbook would discover
little to read on many topics except the historical dic-
tionary or encyclopedia, providing these were available.
For American history to attain the breadth it requires,

an indispensable step is a drastic reorientation in the library's program of acquisitions.

Nor is there an adequate, representative selection of political history. Several items are inevitable standbys: the thin and superseded *Chronicles of America Series,* most of Bruce Catton's books on the Civil War, Mark Sullivan's multivolume *Our Times,* and always the eye-catching but expensive *American Heritage.* The library could ship all these out tomorrow without any great damage to the history course, but it would be much better to add other, more valuable books. Especially pressing is the need to improve the existing holdings in the field of biography, for it is rare indeed to find good lives of Washington, Jefferson, Jackson, Lincoln, Wilson, and other figures of the past. Quite a few libraries have Sandburg's poetic, rambling six-volume study of Lincoln, but not as many have the superb, one-volume biography by Benjamin Thomas.

The average school has a fairly good supply of magazines and newspapers, not always wisely selected but sufficient at least to attract student attention. The local newspaper and often the *New York Times* are available, though the extent of their use declines in that order. Either *Time* or *Newsweek* is on hand for those who may occasionally peek outside the standard weekly newspaper prepared for high schools. Invariably there are home and fashion periodicals appealing to the girls' special interests, while the boys have popular science magazines and their beloved *Sports Illustrated.* One serious deficiency, as a rule, is the absence of the first-rate monthlies, such as *Harper's* and *Atlantic*, which are useful for a wide variety of educational purposes. By and large, teachers are not exploiting these resources as fully as they might. Back files of some magazines, now normally piled up in the storage room, would be much more valuable if they were bound and available on the shelves. The Demco Company has developed an inexpensive process of binding journals with plastic glue and tape.

If the library is going to perform its important function well, very clearly it must order more and better materials. For United States history a desirable beginning would be to obtain most of the volumes in several new sets that are suitable to the course. No doubt the first of these should be the *New American Nation Series*, beginning publication in 1954 and intending to contain forty-three volumes. As experts on their topics, the authors write reliable and yet compact accounts of periods or topics, which will cover the whole distance from colonization to the present. So far about half are in print; and despite a natural variation of quality, most of them reflect the best of recent scholarship and synthesize it in an understandable fashion. Some of the good volumes are Lawrence Henry Gipson's *Coming of the Revolution*, Glyndon G. Van Deusen's *Jacksonian Era*, George E. Mowry's *Era of Theodore Roosevelt*, Arthur S. Link's *Woodrow Wilson and the Progressive Era*, and William E. Leuchtenburg's *Frank-*

lin D. Roosevelt and the New Deal. Each volume has a full, up-to-date bibliography that suggests many other items for further study. Another valuable series is the *Chicago History of American Civilization,* having characteristics similar to the *New American Nation Series* but with more sweep and less depth. Foremost among them are Edmund S. Morgan's *Birth of the Republic, 1763–1789* and Dexter Perkins's *New Age of Franklin Roosevelt, 1932–1945.* Neither set has really caught hold in the high schools.

To meet the perennial problem of arousing interest, an excellent means is to use biographies liberally. But hardly a library has equipped itself as it should in this field. The ideal biography for the high school is one carefully prepared on the basis of primary evidence and vividly written for the nonspecialist. Unfortunately, historians have not always done this. Short biographies with a pleasing style often are superficial, and multivolume ones exhaust the reader as well as the subject. If the librarian and the teacher inform themselves about bibliography and order carefully, however, they will have a reasonably good collection. Van Doren's *Franklin,* Miller's *Hamilton,* James's *Jackson,* Thomas's *Lincoln,* and Pringle's *Theodore Roosevelt* are just the sort of books so urgently required. The pity is that there are not more of them.

Within the past few years a biographical set, in large part fitting these requirements, has appeared. This is the *Library of American Biography,* some volumes of which are still projected though most are now available. Each book is short, under two hundred pages, and smoothly written so that most eleventh graders have no difficulty with it. The authors are quite competent scholars. A majority draw from dependable secondary references and are highly stimulating studies—for example, Current's *Webster* and Nye's *William Lloyd Garrison*. A few, such as Eaton's *Clay*, represent extensive work in the original sources and yet maintain the reader's interest from beginning to end. Inexplicably this series is even more scarce than the others in the schools.

Publishers have increasingly turned to the paperback market. For instance, the three series previously described are also available in that form at half the price of clothbound copies. This means that the cost of a volume is two dollars or less, a genuine bargain nowadays when books are so expensive. These are not abridgments but come off the same typographical plates that print the higher-priced editions, so there can be no substantive objection to them. Nevertheless there has been considerable resistance, particularly from librarians who see special problems of handling and administration. They are less durable, it is said, and require replacement after a few months of hard use. Besides, they are more susceptible to loss or theft since they are small and thin. As a result, not many libraries buy paperbacks in any appreciable quantity; or if they

do, they throw these books together on a special shelf
without catalog numbers or even classifications.

Objections of this nature are unconvincing. Conceding that it may be a significant outlay of time and money
to catalog and maintain items that can fall to pieces
or disappear soon after they arrive, one cannot overlook
the decisive advantages of paperbacks. The initial cost
is small; and if students who might otherwise never
see so many books of this quality and attractiveness
use them, it is good educational accounting to write off
losses and depreciation as well worth while. Moreover
the resourceful librarian can reduce some of the difficulties. It is possible to cover paperbacks with inexpensive
but durable jackets, now available commercially. For
example the New Method Bindery (Jacksonville, Illinois) uses a process costing less than a dollar a copy.
And if necessary, though this is doubtful, the librarian
can merely give the book a broad classification and file
it by author without going through the entire cataloging
process.

Those schools which have sizable budgets for purchasing books will of course order clothbound instead of
paperback copies when both are available. But in many
instances the original editions of works have long been
out of print and have recently reappeared in paperback
only. An example of an old yet very valuable book of
this sort is Frederick Jackson Turner's *Rise of the New
West,* one of several still excellent volumes in the old

American Nation Series (1906), difficult to obtain for many years but reprinted in paperback.

Here and there schools have had heartening success with paperback bookstores. It is usually an official school project with the capital derived from the budget. The profits, which are surprisingly large, support a student activity or serve some other beneficial purpose. As good a purpose as any would be to put the profits into the library fund, and in fact this too has been done. The chief dividends would be to stimulate student reading, to encourage students to acquire books of their own, and to bring students into the library more often to use other books there. In short, a paperback bookstore and the library would be enormously helpful to each other, and both would invigorate the American history course.

Nearly as regrettable as not having a book is not having enough copies. Far too often, indeed almost always, the librarian and the teacher think that when they have ordered one copy they have done their duty. But if a book is important, if the teacher integrates it with classroom instruction as he ought, and if several teachers are concurrently teaching the same course, the library will obviously need multiple copies. Then some can be reserved in the reading room, some can be sent to the classrooms at appropriate times, and there will still be some to circulate. Not many high school students have the hardihood to keep trying to get a book if others are using it each time they search for it. For basic items, such as Randall's *Civil War and Reconstruction*, the librarian should establish a student-book ratio of perhaps twenty-five to one or whatever is a realistic figure determined by experience.

A crucial element in developing the library is the process of ordering. In the main, the librarians bear the full responsibility of selecting which books to acquire. There are a few who look upon this as their prerogative, flowing from a special professional skill, not to be shared by uninformed faculty members who may wreck the budget. In such cases the results are likely to be detrimental academically. But in the preponderant number of schools the librarians are most eager for the teachers to recommend what to order. Usually they request faculty suggestions at least once a year and maybe more often. The response is as feeble as one could imagine. As a matter of fact the typical response is absolute silence. Since most teachers teach American history strictly out of the textbook, neither reading themselves nor asking their students to read, they do not know what the new books are and they do not care.

How, then, does the librarian proceed? If she is alert and industrious, she will follow the cumulative numbers of the *Standard Catalogue for High School Libraries* and check those books especially endorsed by a panel of librarians for United States history. These lists, incidentally, omit a great many of the best books in the field and include others that are next to worthless.

One can understand why this is so, for the persons making the selections simply do not know the subject and have probably not read the books. The average librarian, badly overworked and unfamiliar with the field, however, pursues a more haphazard course in spending her small annual budget. Out of the flurry of publishers' circulars, the visits of book men, and fleeting glances at notices in a library journal or the *Saturday Review* she will devise a makeshift list. The inevitable consequence will be to spend money unwisely, and the history collection will remain inferior. Everyone inclines to castigate the librarian, but the history teacher who has evaded his professional obligation emerges blameless—and bookless too.

There is a state requirement obligating each school to spend a minimum amount per student for its library. Though it is a bit difficult to reconstruct what actually occurs, there are indications that many schools do not in fact comply with the spirit and perhaps with the letter of this rule. The policy depends first of all upon the school board or the trustees to provide the money, and then upon the librarian. She may spend more than justified for physical improvements or clerical assistance and not enough for buying books. More often she succumbs to the temptation of purchasing expensive audiovisual materials, which she might more practically borrow or rent, though she will tell the inquirer that this comes from a separate fund. If so, some of that fund ought to go into the book budget rather than the reverse.

Or she may subscribe to more costly encyclopedias and ephemeral slick magazines than she can afford. Although these financial matters are sometimes a reason for the lack of progress, they are certainly not the main reason. If the teachers know what they need and insist upon it with even a little determination, they will get it. Money goes elsewhere principally by default of those who should be using it.

Unquestionably the library will have a sound, intelligent order program only if the teachers assume an active role. Each faculty member must become acquainted with the standard literature of American history and must have the habit as well as the means of learning about the new books as they appear. Furthermore he must use these books in his instruction not only to justify the expenditure of funds but also to assist his students as they read. This is time-consuming, demanding work, but there is no painless way. For one thing the teacher should come into the library more often than he does in order to see what the library has and what his students are doing there. By so informing himself he will have a clearer idea of what is needed.

A number of systematic measures are available. The librarian, and most teachers personally, should acquire bibliographical guides in American history and consult them before ordering. An indispensable item is the *Harvard Guide to American History*, which will serve very well to identify the older books (published before 1954) that the library should hold. Lists and comments in up-to-date college textbooks (the newest edition of Morison and Commager's *Growth of the American Republic,* for instance) and in such series as the *New American Nation* are very full. Indiana University's Lilly Program in American History has prepared *Books in American History: A Basic List for Schools* (Indiana University Press, 1964; $1.00). And for current publications nothing is as good as the *Mississippi Valley Historical Review,* now called *The Journal of American History.* All high school libraries, large and small, should subscribe to this magazine, obviously for this bibliographical purpose and for other purposes as well. *The Journal of American History* is one of the best ways, incidentally, for the teacher to keep abreast of the recent findings and interpretations of historical scholars; and it is useful to superior students for advanced reading and written reports. There is no shortage of readily accessible aids to compile an order list as lengthy as the school's resources permit.

A special problem exists when books are out of print. Normally publishers exhaust their stock of monographs and biographies after a few years and can no longer supply these items. Numerous newly constructed schools, particularly those consolidating several small rural districts as well as the burgeoning junior highs everywhere, feel the difficulty of the problem acutely. They must begin building their libraries from nothing and may assemble an unbalanced collection lacking much of the standard literature. In part, such schools can avoid this if they order the paperback reprints now on the market. The librarian can also obtain most out-of-print volumes from book dealers, though of course she will not wish to pay the exorbitant prices they ask for some "rare" books.

The skeptic will inquire how all this is possible for a typical library struggling along as it does on a modest budget provided by the tightfisted school board. Of course, even with unlimited funds, developing a library is a long-range, painstaking project, so no one should become discouraged if, after two or three years, the book collection has enormous gaps. More than money is necessary to put together an adequate library. But money helps. Administrators and faculty—principal, librarian, and teachers—should think of the library as the academic center of the school, the intellectual laboratory for all the students. And they should attempt to convince the superintendent, the school board, and the community to look upon it in the same way. In most instances, the determinant will be the transformation of the library into the vital ingredient of the instructional program, for then the desirability of giving it every encouragement will have meaning to the budget makers. Though there may be resistance, it cannot last long in these circumstances.

The sad truth is that the library is not presently the intellectual center of most schools. The average student reads little beyond his textbook, he does not think of library work as part of his history course, and he does not clearly understand the fundamental purpose of the library. Year after year, many teachers make no suggestions for ordering, never visit the library, and do not have the slightest interest in it. In such schools it really does not matter what books are on hand or what the librarian plans to acquire, for they will lie unused.

As enrollments rapidly increase and school buildings become overcrowded, there is a decided tendency to invade the library for the space it can provide. One well-known practice is using it as a study hall, and in conditions at their worst a school may do this every period of the day. Obviously the consequence is to waste the most valuable space in the whole building, because while these students sit there and read their textbooks or do nothing or "cut up," they are occupying places that ought to be available to others for library work. Some observers will argue that the space would otherwise be vacant; but that is begging the question, for teachers should see that the library is not vacant. Frequently the room is a social gathering spot, not only during free periods but at almost any hour when students can too easily check out of a study hall or classroom and go to the library with no serious goal in mind. They may catch up on their favorite popular magazines, visit with their friends, or find other diversion. In any case, the librarian becomes a custodian, saddled with disciplinary problems, whereas she should be devoting her time and skill to more constructive ends. Usually she has little assistance and may have to serve as her own stenographer, desk attendant, or shelver, or all of them combined. When she depletes her energies in this fashion, she cannot do those things she has been trained to do.

It is misleading to give the impression that all librarians are the epitome of virtue and talent, however much as a group they deserve sympathetic understanding. In small schools a teacher of English or some other subject may draw the added assignment of tending the library, though he may know very little about performing the duties and may not particularly care to learn. Such part-time, untrained librarians are seldom able to fulfill their responsibilities. There are also some, but fortunately not many, trained librarians who should be doing something else. These persons are utterly disinterested in books, or so fond of possessing them that they are reluctant to see them used. Thus their policy is to close the room to readers as soon as the bell sounds for the lunch hour or afternoon dismissal. They make it difficult to find and charge out books, and all the while their demeanor is so forbidding that students have to be brave indeed to venture into the library. Persons of this kind, however, are a small minority of the whole number of dedicated, industrious librarians; and they are probably a disappearing breed. At least one hopes so.

The most necessary reform of high school libraries is to coordinate their functions with classroom work. This is primarily the teacher's responsibility. He must know his library and constantly seek to improve it not merely by helping to select new books, important as this is, but by getting the books into his students' hands. His course should be a challenging enterprise in reading and not a drill to assure the memorization of the text-book. Accordingly his students will think of the library as a place where they study the subject rather than as a place where they grudgingly go to pacify the instructor. Early in the school year the teacher should take his whole class to the library, no doubt more than once, and help them learn how to use reference works, how to find the sort of books they wish, and how generally to conduct themselves there. His rapport with the librarian should be close so that by his knowledge of the library's policies and practices he can better counsel his students. This close relationship will also facilitate changes he thinks essential.

Several specific procedures have proved useful to those teachers who have collaborated with their librarians. One is to set aside a section in the library for new or particularly significant publications in the field of American history. These can circulate or remain on reserve as circumstances require. Another is to charge a cartful of books to the classroom for greater convenience of study. As the year progresses, other books will replace them; but a number of basic references should always be near the teacher's desk. Quite possibly books may occasionally be lost or stolen, but common-sense precautions will reduce these to negligible proportions.

Besides if there are some losses, the price is not too high to pay in terms of the educational value. Nothing should unduly interfere with the students' access to the books and with their privilege of withdrawing them for home use. Unless they can read outside school hours, they will not learn very much.

Although there are encouraging signs that a good many people realize how badly the libraries need a thorough overhaul, and although some schools have made a beginning, few have attained minimal standards. Even a librarian with infinite patience and wisdom can finish only part of the task. What the teacher does is decisive.

6 | THE OUTER WORLD

If the classroom is a small world presided over by the teacher, what then of the outer world—outer space, one might describe it? What of the lunar and solar systems, the constellations, the milky way perhaps, all the surroundings in terms of people and organizations which affect the classroom? What of this world of principals, department heads, assistant superintendents and superintendents, parents, school boards, and other nameless persons and organizations?

The principal is clearly the most important non-classroom factor entering the discourse between students and teacher, and deserves a close look by anyone seeking

108

to ensure standards in the teaching of American history in the high schools. The principals of high schools are about the same everywhere. They are products of the local school system, almost always teachers who have come up through the ranks. Many have been former coaches. It is difficult to know the percentage of former coaches or industrial arts teachers who have become principals; there are no clear statistics. Probably the number is very high, well over fifty per cent. One might have expected such a result, for the former coaches or shop teachers are gregarious types, who easily meet the public and have ability at organization. Often they are insecure in their classroom teaching, especially the coaches, and drift toward the principal's office. As for other men who have become principals, some have taught longer than their fellows. A few teachers have turned to administration because of the money; for anyone holding down the principal's chair there is a fair-sized increase in salary, perhaps two or three thousand dollars.

One thing is certain about a principal's job: it requires a great deal of time. It gives little chance for contemplation and quiet reading. The principal is the head of a busy enterprise in an age of easy communication and transportation—telephones, cars. Around the school there are many chores such as counting cafeteria money, communicating with occasional carpenters and repairmen of all sorts, etc. etc. Everything tends to come down on the principal. There also are the outside activities. The principal probably must belong to one of the community service clubs. He probably will be active in a church. In a large town or city it is easier to keep away from the out-of-school activities. In a small town or township school the principal is expected to be the working wheel in many affairs. It is a rare occasion when in leisure he can take a book off the shelf and read it, savoring its ideas and literary expression. He finds almost no time in the day for such occupation. Reading has to be at night, and there is little time then.

This is not to say that the average principal is anti-intellectual, but that he is nonintellectual. By intellectual one does not speak of an individual who busies himself reading numerous volumes each year and writing a book on some esoteric subject. One means a person who has time to read, say, a book a week. If one could take a census of book reading among principals, it would show little reading. The principal is not against learning; far from it. He is not, though, enough of a reader to understand the delicate intellectual problems of a school. Both the solution of intellectual difficulties of the moment within his school and the larger problems of innovation are likely to be beyond his initiative.

One should remark that a principal must have a special principal's license, a requirement which tends further to reduce the intellectuality of public school administrators. A principal's license requires hours of courses in how to run a school. These are method rather than subject-matter courses, strictly the business of "how to do it." Usually a would-be principal will take his master's degree within the field of education rather than the subject-matter departments. And many principals have already taken much of their undergraduate instruction in education rather than subject-matter fields. As James D. Koerner points out in *The Miseducation of American Teachers,* "The staffing of key administrative posts in public schools with persons whose academic training sometimes stops after the sophomore undergraduate year in college and rarely extends to graduate work in any liberal arts field is hardly the way to strengthen the intellectual life of these schools; indeed it is an excellent way to enfeeble it."

The principal therefore is likely to make the same mistake as many teachers, namely, to comprehend his work of supervisor of teachers as being a process, keeping order, organization, without understanding the essential task of a school—which is to impart as much of the world's learning to students as possible within the confines of the average school day and homework in the evenings and on week ends.

In light of the above it is interesting to observe the attitude of teachers toward their principals—a mixture of naïve regard, of genuine appreciation, and of annoyance. Inexperienced teachers often think the principal has possession of the keys to the kingdom, ability to open gates to the great beyond. As for teachers not in awe, many respect and appreciate their supervisors, especially if the principal backs them on disciplinary problems; also, when a teacher has an idea for improving the classroom performance and finds the principal willing to use all the engines of the school to forward the idea, it is an exhilarating experience, and the teacher is deeply grateful. Unfortunately, it is necessary to add that there is a good deal of annoyance with principals. This is naturally a *sub rosa* situation. Many older teachers are "fed up" with the principal, having seen young whippersnappers with little experience in the classroom get into the principal's office and, sooner or later, into situations where the newcomers are telling the old-timers how to teach. There is an average amount of sheer grousing by teachers against supervisors who cannot always agree with suggestions from the ranks. There nonetheless is a considerable amount, larger than one would think, of general criticism of principals by the teachers—criticism that the principal "doesn't know his job," that he is a nonreader, almost nonverbal, a consumer of chicken salad at outside luncheons, a fellow who likes to snooze in his private office, who is unwilling or unable (or both) to act or advise.

Perhaps the chief complaint against the principals, a justifiable one, is that they often let intellectual things slide as long as there is no trouble. The principals often show a distinct lack of academic leadership. An outside observer can see principals with a desire to run

an impeccably organized school—and most of the schools
do run like clockwork—but inability to look beyond the
floor wax and attendance figures. Many teachers have
no administrative aspirations, enjoy teaching, wish only
to have helpful guidance in their work. For them it is
unnerving to be in complete control of a classroom, any
classroom, where—so any teacher of merit soon comes
to feel—there is a subtle and ever-changing situation, a
terribly delicate affair of the intellect. Instruction from
a master teacher in control of the administrative
machinery of the school would be of great value.

As for other administrative officers of the average
school, individuals to whom the teacher of American
history might go to change a course outline or a textbook, there is virtually no one but the department head.
The department head is likely to be a frail reed. Departments are largely artificial creations, in imitation of
college and university departments. They relieve the
principal's office of paperwork and in that sense are
useful. They give recognition to senior members of the
high school staff. They simplify, or seem to simplify, the
business of visiting the classes of teachers who are without tenure or otherwise in doubtful status. The department heads have little authority and often little
ability and cannot help the teacher seeking advice on
classroom problems.

Nor do superintendents of schools or their subordi-
nates have much part in the average teaching situation.
In small schools the superintendent is important. In

large city systems he is a shadow. There may be superficial contact through an occasional statesmanlike address, but nothing more. His several supervisors—assistant superintendents or the specialist-supervisors—except for an occasional well-advertised visit likewise have little importance in the classroom.

The parents, one might suppose, could act as a classroom force, if only because they hear reports of progress or regress each night when children come home from school. Yet seldom is such the case. The average teacher has little contact with parents. Students are not eager to have parents mousing around the school. If by chance a student does not object when his parents presume to enter the classroom equation then his fellows may taunt him into objecting, in the way children so effectively discipline each other. The parents, however, are not anxious anyway to interfere in the schools. They have heard a great deal about the schoolteacher as a professional person, and they tend to think a member of a profession is wise enough to control his own business. "Would I want someone to come down and tell me how to run my business?" Unless a student is doing badly in school, parents seldom talk at length and intimately with the teacher. Complaints from the teacher are revealing on this score.

Efforts to organize a worthwhile parent-teacher relationship have almost uniformly broken down when confronted with parental reluctance. The administration in a given school may or may not dominate the

P.T.A., but the parents often think it does. The parents
give up before they start. The P.T.A. becomes a polite
bore, wasting time in discussion, spending what energies it can generate in collecting money for new band
uniforms. Once a year the parents "look in on" the
classroom; but they are too self-conscious or their
children are too self-conscious to make anything more
than a show out of the annual evening during American
Education Week when the children, like circus animals,
perform.

It is a pity that such is the case, for teacher testimony
is unanimous as to the force which a few parents, organized or not, can exert within a school. Parents have
enormous power in the average school, if they will use
it. A principal is apt to put much more weight on the
comments of a few disgruntled parents than on the
pleased silence of the remainder. If a parent is willing
to face down a principal, or an offending teacher, he can
accomplish great things with little exertion. Even the
P.T.A., much maligned, can be a marvelous source of
pressure.

But here is this present-day situation, for better or
worse. Lacking pressure from outside, the teacher is
pretty much in charge. Whatever he says goes, within
reasonable limits. The principal almost never visits the
classroom although he may tune in surreptitiously on
the intercom ("my classroom," one teacher said, "is
bugged"). The department head will watch a beginning, nontenure teacher, but soon leave him on his

own. The superintendent's office is a cipher. Parents are not in evidence.

What can correct this state of affairs? What people, ideas, acts can interpose themselves in the far too restricted classroom equation? As mentioned, many teachers find their authority in class embarrassing and would like to have contact with the outer world, serious guidance from the principal, criticism (which may, like all criticism, be favorable or unfavorable) from parents. Again, for varying reasons parents and principals are unlikely to do great things in bucking up sagging school systems. Can rank "outsiders"—say, people in the universities, or the general public, who desire to raise intellectual standards in the public schools—do anything?

Fortunately there are some levers available to persons who wish to be helpful. School boards are a major source of change, or can be, if they realize their power. It would be necessary for the average board to raise its sights, to move out of the confinements of cafeteria management, of paint and varnish and the ten thousand other things which enter into operating a typical school. Many boards, sensitive to money and sound business management, rightly want to know how the physical end of schools is going. Members feel that they understand this sort of thing from their daily lives and that in this respect they can make a contribution. It may also be that the average principal or superintendent likes the board to take interest in physical problems. The school administrator, unsure of the intellectual side of his work, prefers that the sharp, intelligent men and women of the board keep off classroom subjects. And discussion of intellectual problems might involve going to one of the teachers and asking his opinion, which would be bad administration for it would cut out the administrator, that essential link between teacher and board. The average school board could play a large role in a system by making short shrift of mechanical matters, even letting a few dollars go down the drain, and dealing with the intellectual development of the children.

There are other levers for school improvement, one of which entails a return of public school leadership to academic departments of the state colleges or universities. It is an old story of how at the turn of the twentieth century, when public education was becoming a large affair involving millions of students and tens of thousands of teachers, the colleges and universities abdicated their responsibility and farmed out—or allowed to be farmed out—the training of teachers to teachers' colleges or, within the larger universities, to departments and schools of education. The time has now come, as most university professors of history will testify, when supervision of high school teaching of history should return to the academic faculties. Members of present-day faculties had no part in the curricular delinquencies of their predecessors of fifty or sixty years ago.

Incidentally, one should remark that the average

teacher of history in a college or university must do more than talk about poor high school teaching. It does no good to lament the illiteracies of college freshmen— to point out that these beautifully dressed, well-mannered young adults, such obviously cultivated young ladies and gentlemen, cannot spell their own language or compose coherent paragraphs, that they have read little in books of quality and have no fund of metaphor and simile and know hardly anything about the world outside their community except as it appears in television or the movies. At a time when college enrollments are climbing rapidly, when there are not enough trained college instructors to go around, when the college teacher has no time to finish off the high school education of his students, it is idle for him to complain in the faculty lounge about student illiteracies. He must make the problems of high school teaching his serious personal concern. He must undertake to help high school students and teachers, in every way possible, even if it interferes with his cherished research and writing.

It should be, though, a comforting thought to the concerned college instructor that today's rapidly increasing college enrollments offer, for the first time, an excellent opportunity for him to couple good deeds with his good thoughts. The instructor of times past who wished to be not merely vocal but helpful in improving high school curricula often concluded quickly that there was nothing much he could do. His good

intentions sometimes led to an invitation to an educational workshop—a talkfest. Or he disguised his own
courses as a workshop, hoping to entice some high
school teachers into his intellectual bear traps. But it was
slow work in anybody's workshop. Happily, things now
have changed. The college instructor should be able to
take measures within his university which will assert
university leadership of the high school curriculum. By
raising college standards he can raise high school standards. At the present writing nearly half the high school
population is going on to college. High school students
are having all sorts of traumatic experiences trying to
get into the major colleges and universities. No longer
do colleges have to "fill the dorms." Each college instructor should be able to insist on minimum performance of the literacies—reading, writing, and spelling. If
an incoming student does not show these primeval
talents the student should go into a remedial class,
receive "X" credit (no credit), and pay a giant-sized
fee for the privilege of getting this remedial "X" credit.
The result will be immediate pressure on every local
public school which offers inadequate instruction.

The college instructor also can use the advanced-
placement test, mentioned in an earlier chapter.

There are many obstacles to reform. It would be
foolish of anyone, and terribly disappointing, to think
otherwise. It will be no easy task to pierce the murk
and narrowness of pedantic high school courses in
American history. People today are so busy, and they

hesitate to take on difficult new jobs. Erring school administrators often can control a discussion by a few bold assertions. To the anxious professor of history there is the reassurance that a school's history teachers are the best possible. Or if there are a few things wrong, by and large affairs are in good shape. A frequent obstacle to change is, queerly enough, the fact that schools undoubtedly have improved over the years and that the instruction today is generally better than it was twenty years ago, not to mention forty or sixty years. Anyone favoring change has to face the commentary that improvement is undeniable and that "there will be more, just be patient." A conversation also can shift easily to hints about the peculiarly "ivory tower" incompetence of university critics. There was an edge to the apparently friendly remark of a high school principal to one of the authors of this book: "Well, well, how are you, Dr. ———? It is Doctor, isn't it? We really are glad for you to come here and observe our system, for we need ideas from you people in the universities. What ideas do you have for us today?"

Despite such obstacles it is high time to change much of the teaching of American history in high school. In our apocalyptic second half of the twentieth century too many things are at stake to allow inefficient learning. The placid routines of many American history classrooms are far too slow for today's pace of life. Our contemporary era has seen almost incessant crisis. Never in human annals have such large events tumbled over each other so fast. It is easily possible to show how recent complications have dwarfed the great historic crises of the past—the fall of Rome, the Renaissance and Reformation, the French Revolution, the Tai-ping Rebellion, even the First and Second World Wars. These crises are now moving downward in historic importance as compared to the hectic present and the ominous future. Both for Americans as individuals and for their country it is a dangerous time to continue allowing the nation's students to graduate from high school with so little knowledge or appreciation of American history.

7 | STATISTICAL SURVEY

As noted in the foreword of this book, the authors gathered information and ideas about American history teaching in Indiana in several ways. They and four colleagues toured the state over a three-year period, visited more than seventy junior and senior high schools, observed classes, examined libraries, talked with teachers, students, librarians, principals, superintendents. They scrutinized credentials of 275 teachers who applied for Indiana University's Lilly Fellowships in American History, had many informal conversations with the 152 successful applicants during their summers at Indiana University in the years 1961–64, attended a workshop and conferences in which teachers wrestled with curriculum revision, discussed a range of questions pertinent to history teaching with members of Indiana University's School of Education and with faculty members of other colleges and universities in the state. During the summer of 1963 they interviewed 200 teachers of American history, asking a variety of questions about teacher habits, students, the American history course, the classroom, libraries, administrators.

Then there was the questionnaire survey of November 1963–January 1964. After attempting to identify every teacher of American history and high school librarian in the state, the authors made a "saturation" survey, sending questionnaires to all teachers and librarians. Individuals with experience in the questionnaire technique of gathering information warned that it is usually difficult to secure even a 30 per cent return. But thanks to the persistence of Lilly program secretaries, especially Meridel Scherer Rawlins, and the goodwill and interest of Indiana's teachers and librarians, the percentage of return on both the teacher and librarian questionnaires was unusually high. The teacher questionnaire had a return of 80 per cent— 1,084 out of 1,353. The librarian questionnaire did even better—85 per cent—564 out of 665.

The teacher questionnaire sought information on the teacher's educational background. Where did he get his bachelor's degree? Was his degree in history or education or something else? How many semester hours of history did he have as an undergraduate? As a graduate? How many hours in education? The questionnaire asked teachers for an opinion on the value of work in history and education. It sought accurate information on the percentage of American history teachers who are coaches. It also inquired the years teachers had taught American history in grade school and high school.

The survey checked into the teacher's daily routine and extracurricular responsibilities—hours spent daily in the classroom, number of history classes taught daily, other subjects taught, attendance at parent-teacher meetings, supervision of study halls, sponsorship of school clubs.

There was the matter of intellectual activity. What are the teacher's reading habits? Does he try to keep abreast of historical scholarship? Does he know books in American history? What has he read in the field in the past year? Does he consider his reading sufficient for effective teaching?

The survey sought information on the student. It asked for opinions on the most popular and least popular parts of the American history course, and sought an estimate of student interest in American history. There was a question on homework assigned and time spent on homework. Another asked the teacher to estimate the percentage of students from his school who go to college. Another asked if the teacher's school took into account differences in student ability.

The teacher questionnaire asked about the American

history course and classroom. Does the teacher emphasize chronology or topics? What textbook does he use? How closely does the course follow the organization of the textbook? Does the teacher have trouble finishing the course? What does he require beyond the textbook? What, if any, audiovisual aids does he use? How does the teacher use the class period? How does he treat current events? Does the school use educational television? What kind of examinations does the teacher ordinarily give? How much outside reading does he require?

The teacher questionnaire asked about cooperation of the librarian and the teacher's part in ordering books. But most information on libraries came from the separate questionnaire to librarians. The librarian questionnaire asked if the library had its own room—apart from the study hall. It sought information on the age of school libraries and the number of books, asked librarians for opinions on utilization of libraries and the adequacy of present library facilities. It inquired the number of books in American history, the number of history books ordered in the previous year, interest by American history teachers in ordering books, use of library by students in the American history course. The questionnaire asked about the distance from school of public libraries. Then there were questions on the library budget and the budget for audiovisual aids.

The teacher questionnaire had items on the so-called "outer world." How much supervision does the teacher receive? What about pressure by administrators, patriotic organizations, parents, civic groups to avoid "sensitive" topics in American history? How much interest do school administrators show in the handling of the American history course? Do parents show interest?

One might note that much labor went into the business of compiling data from questionnaires. Over a three-month period two to five secretaries kept busy tabulating, coding, validating. Next, the Indiana University computing center punched the data on cards. Finally, in a grand climax that consumed only a few minutes, a giant computer made several hundred thousand calculations and belched forth results presented in this chapter.

It is important to add that the authors have reservations concerning results of this survey. They do not pretend that it provides a scientific base for conclusions set forth in this book. It was clear in some instances that answers were rather wild guesses. Some questions caused honest confusion. And where the questionnaires had built-in validity checks, results demonstrated the technique's limited reliability. Results of this survey, indeed, have shown inherent weaknesses of questionnaire surveys—so much in vogue nowadays. The authors believe that their observations in the schools and conversations with teachers and students conveyed in some ways a more accurate picture of the teaching of American history in Indiana's high schools.

Results of the survey follow.

1. THE TEACHER

Where did Indiana's American history teachers receive undergraduate training? As one travels about the state this question pops up frequently. The survey provided several small surprises. First, only 15 per cent of the teachers hold bachelor's degrees from Indiana University, despite the size of its history department and School of Education. Twenty-nine per cent took undergraduate training at other public colleges and universities in the state. Most people in this category listed Ball State College and Indiana State College. A surprisingly large number—39 per cent—reported degrees from private schools in Indiana—DePauw, Butler, Wabash, Indiana Central, Hanover, Earlham, Notre Dame. Only a handful—7 per cent—had degrees from public institutions outside Indiana. Ten per cent reported degrees from non-Indiana private schools. Broken down another way, this shows that 83 per cent of Indiana's American history teachers received undergraduate training in Indiana, a high figure, it would seem, in this era of mobile populations. As between public and private institutions, 51 per cent had taken bachelor's degrees from public schools.

One also hears considerable discussion about the kind of degrees held by teachers. The survey showed that 34 per cent of Indiana's American history teachers hold bachelor's degrees in history, a higher percentage than the authors anticipated but far below what they think desirable. Forty-five per cent reported a bachelor's degree in education. Surprising perhaps was the number—21 per cent—who reported that they had received an undergraduate degree in neither history nor education.

The authors doubt the reliability of figures regarding undergraduate and graduate hours in history and education. There obviously was a good deal of confusion over semester hours and quarter hours. Then several hundred interviews and conversations with teachers have shown a tendency for teachers to consider as history all work in "social studies." The questionnaire, moreover, asked the teacher to reach back into his memory—in some cases quite a few years—and come forth with accurate figures. Hazards of such procedure are apparent. A careful sampling of teacher transcripts would yield more accurate data.

As for undergraduate hours in history, the survey reported that only 3 per cent of the teachers of American history had fewer than ten semester hours of work in history, only 15 per cent fewer than twenty hours. Thirty-nine per cent reported between twenty and twenty-nine hours, 22 per cent between thirty and thirty-nine, 19 per cent between forty and forty-nine. Five per cent reported fifty hours or more. Such figures, if approximately accurate, indicate that most Indiana teachers of American history did a fair amount of undergraduate work in history, although, one must note, much of it doubtless was in non-American areas. Only 40 per cent—too many, to be sure, but fewer than expected—reported fewer than twenty-five semester hours, the minimum for an undergraduate major in history at most colleges and universities.

Regarding undergraduate work in education, 7 per cent of Indiana's American history teachers reported fewer than ten semester hours, 43 per cent reported between ten and nineteen hours, 36 per cent between twenty and twenty-nine. Fourteen per cent reported thirty or more undergraduate hours in education. These figures indicate that the typical teacher has taken fewer undergraduate courses in education than critics often assume. Whether it is desirable that half the American history teachers of the state have more than twenty hours of work in education (more than is required for licensing) at the expense of work in the so-called "subject area" is an open question.

How about graduate work? The survey disclosed that many American history teachers have not begun pursuit of a master's degree or have made slight headway. Figures showed that 30 per cent of the teachers have not taken a single graduate course in history and another 30 per cent have taken between one and nine semester hours of history. Another 18 per cent have completed between ten and nineteen hours. Since twenty hours of history is the minimum for an M.A. degree in history at most universities, these figures indicate that 78 per cent of Indiana's American history teachers have not taken enough hours for such a degree. The percentage doubtless is much higher, since only 774—of the

1,084—gave a response to this question. Eleven per cent have taken between twenty and twenty-nine hours of history. Another 11 per cent have taken thirty hours or more—the amount of work taken by many M.A. candidates in history at Indiana University. A rather surprising total of 21 per cent of the teachers reported no graduate work in education. Twenty-four per cent have completed one to nine hours, 23 per cent ten to nineteen, 15 per cent twenty to twenty-nine. Seventeen per cent of the American history teachers have taken thirty or more graduate hours of education. Again one should note that only 732 questionnaires showed a response to this question. Although these figures do not disclose hours in other fields—economics, sociology, geography, literature—they reveal a preference for graduate work in education. As noted in Chapter 1, the authors believe that graduate work in education does little for the classroom teacher, that most of the history teacher's work should be in history and related subjects.

Making this finding on graduate work in education more interesting—and giving support to the authors' views—were teacher responses on the relative value to them, as teachers, of work in education and history. Only 18 per cent considered most of their work in education essential to making them good secondary teachers. Seventy-eight per cent reported that the majority of their courses in history were essential in making them good teachers. Fifty-four per cent believed that most of their work in education had been helpful though not essential in making them good teachers. Twenty per cent thought their work in history helpful but not essential. Twenty-four per cent thought their work in education of little use in making them good teachers, only 2 per cent considered their work in history of little use. Four per cent thought their work in education of no use, 0.2 per cent thought their work in history of no use. Despite this overwhelming sentiment in favor of history, many American history teachers continue to emphasize education in graduate school.

Years in the classroom are an important part of the teacher's background. The survey disclosed that 62 per cent of Indiana's high school teachers of American history also have taught in elementary schools. Indeed, 11 per cent have taught elementary school from ten to nineteen years, and 3 per cent have taught more than twenty years in elementary school. As for years teaching American history in high school, the survey revealed that 68 per cent of Indiana's American history teachers have taught less than ten years. Eighteen per cent have taught between ten and nineteen years, 14 per cent twenty years or more. These figures indicate that a great many young people—under age thirty-five—are teaching American history. They also indicate that many experienced teachers for one reason or another have left the American history classroom in the past decade.

As noted in Chapter 1, a view having wide currency is that athletic coaches are heavily involved in American history teaching, and some people voice the view that most American history teachers are coaches. This survey revealed that more than two thirds of Indiana's American history teachers have no involvement in coaching. Six per cent do some coaching in minor sports—golf, tennis, sixth-grade basketball. Only 25 per cent of the American history teachers coach "major" high school sports—football and basketball. Considering that the coach seldom teaches more than one or two sections of American history, the authors believe it accurate to say that no more than 20 per cent (and probably somewhat fewer) of Indiana's history students are under teachers whose first responsibility and interest is coaching.

The authors wanted to learn something about teaching assignments and loads of individuals responsible for American history in Indiana's high schools—different courses taught, hours spent in the classroom, hours spent teaching American history. Two per cent failed to respond to the question asking teachers to list different courses taught daily. Sixteen per cent reported that they teach one course only, 35 per cent reported two different courses, 27 per cent three, 12 per cent four, 6 per cent five, and 2 per cent six different courses. As for kinds of courses taught by American history teachers, 15 per cent reported that they teach nothing but American history— a discouraging figure, considering that American history, a compulsory course in high school, usually requires several sections. Thirty-nine per cent reported that they teach American history and other "social studies"—

world history, government, economics, geography. This
means that barely over half of Indiana's American history teachers work only in history and related fields.
Twelve per cent teach American history and courses
not classed as social studies, 9 per cent have assignments
that include American history and physical education,
14 per cent teach American history, other social studies,
and courses not considered social studies, 9 per cent
are not teaching American history at all. Two per cent
failed to respond. The survey also sought information
on the number of sections of American history taught
by the individual teacher. Twenty-three per cent teach
only one section, 30 per cent two, 17 per cent three,
11 per cent four, 8 per cent five sections, and 1 per cent
six. As mentioned, 9 per cent of the teachers are not
teaching American history at the moment. One per cent
did not respond.

How many hours does the teacher spend in the classroom daily? Here is another question that generates
discussion. This survey disclosed that 5 per cent of the
American history teachers spend one or two hours a day
in the classroom, obviously dividing their time between
teaching and other responsibilities. Five per cent are in
the classroom three hours daily, 18 per cent four hours,
56 per cent five, 15 per cent six, and 1 per cent seven.
As for the length of the classroom period, there was
a surprising spread. Six per cent of the teachers reported that their classes run forty minutes, 1 per
cent reported forty-five-minute periods, 9 per cent

have fifty-minute classes, 74 per cent have fifty-five minutes, 6 per cent sixty, and 4 per cent more than sixty. Asked about teaching load, 1 per cent of the teachers thought their load too light. The surprising answer, in view of complaints one hears, was from the 63 per cent who thought their teaching load "about right." Only 36 per cent regarded their teaching load too heavy.

The survey sought to determine nonclassroom, school-related activities of American history teachers. Results showed that 85 per cent attend parent-teacher meetings, 86 per cent state teachers conferences, 78 per cent have attended summer college classes, 64 per cent night school or taken correspondence courses, 91 per cent read professional teacher magazines, 6 per cent have taken travel tours for college credit. Since one hears a good deal about compulsory extra-teaching duties, the survey sought some precise information. It revealed that only 28 per cent of the American history teachers must attend parent-teacher meetings, only 49 per cent must attend sporting events, dances, auditorium programs. A larger percentage—80 per cent—reported such responsibilities as supervising study halls, cafeterias, parking lots, hallways. Fifty-one per cent reported that schools required them to sponsor school clubs or the school paper.

In the authors' view the most interesting part of the teacher survey touched upon the intellectual interests of teachers of American history. As noted in Chapter 1, the authors contend that failure of teachers to take large interest in the literature of history is a basic obstacle to effective classroom instruction. Since they feared that teachers might be reluctant to state accurately their recent intellectual activity, the authors felt compelled to include validity checks in this part of the survey. There was no intention to make teachers appear ridiculous or untruthful. But since this was such an important part of the survey—and since there was a wide margin for erroneous reporting—there had to be checks. This is standard in the questionnaire technique.

On one item the authors asked teachers to list books in American history they had read in the past year. Many teachers listed two or three high school textbooks. There is strong reason to doubt that any teacher waded through several high school textbooks. This generous listing of textbooks, moreover, made the authors suspicious of listings of non-textbooks. At any rate, since textbooks do not present serious intellectual challenges—and since they are not repositories of new ideas and interpretations—the authors dismissed them when totaling responses to this question. After one has discounted textbooks, then, he finds that 52 per cent of the teachers reported no books in American history read over the past year. Another 35 per cent had read fewer than six books—certainly not a great amount of reading in history. Only 7 per cent reported that they had read ten or more books in American history in the previous year, and, we might add, a large number of this group (the titles listed gave them away) clearly were teachers involved in the Lilly program of reading, in which these books were assigned.

As a footnote to this part of the survey, the authors totaled the listing of books by Bruce Catton, the well-known historian of the Civil War. Eleven per cent of the teachers had read something by Catton in the past year, 3 per cent reporting more than one of his books.

In another part of the survey there were listed ten authors and titles, and the teacher was to check Column A if he had read the book and Column B if he had not read but had heard of the book. Since it is easy enough to make a check mark, it was necessary to have a validity check here. Hence five of the ten books listed do not exist. Fictitious books bore little or no resemblance to real books. Results in percentage of responses were as follows:

	Column A (read)	Column B (heard of)
Arthur M. Schlesinger, Jr., *The Coming of the New Deal*	39	39
Edwin N. Kaufman, *America and the Frst World War**	14	32
Robert M. Shaw, *A Biography of Old Hickory**	17	27
Allan Nevins, *Ordeal of the Union*	24	32
Gerhard Engelmeier, *The American Immigrant**	9	24
Roberta Wohlstetter, *Pearl Harbor: Warning and Decision*	20	28
Leslie H. Hawkins, *Columbus**	7	20
Harold Stevenson Robards, *Slavery and the Civil War**	21	26
Walter Lord, *The Good Years*	27	33
Frederick Lewis Allen, *Only Yesterday*	33	25

* Fictitious book

The computer disclosed that 37 per cent of the teachers reported the reading of one or more fictitious books, 56 per cent reported that they had heard of a fictitious book: 17 per cent had "read" one of them, 12 per cent two, 6 per cent three, 2 per cent four, and less than 1 per cent five. No doubt some teachers confused fictitious titles with books they had read in the distant past. One has to allow for a margin of unavoidable error. But it is clear that many teachers did not deal seriously with this question.

The authors, therefore, had reason to doubt the accuracy of responses concerning real books. If individuals checked fictitious books, it is just as likely that they checked real books without having read them. Then there were the results showing that 39 per cent of the teachers had read the volume by Schlesinger, 24 per cent the work (a six-volume affair) by Nevins. Though these are well-written books, the authors find it incredible—in view of their observation of teacher reading habits—that so many people have read these books. The Wohlstetter book provides better support for this view. Mrs. Wohlstetter's book came out in 1962, but did not receive review in scholarly or popular periodicals until 1963. Hence if a teacher read Wohlstetter it is almost certain that he read it in the year 1963 or early 1964. The questionnaire, as mentioned, went out in the period November 1963—January 1964. Thus if the teacher had read Wohlstetter and checked Wohlstetter on this part of the questionnaire, he should have listed it on the earlier item which asked teachers to list books in American history read within the past year. A total of 220 teachers checked Column A that they read the Wohlstetter book. Only six indicated on the earlier question that they had read Wohlstetter within the past year.

Perhaps results of this part of the survey demonstrate that the American history teacher knows what kind of image he ought to project—a person who reads books. That history teachers in Indiana may know this is an encouraging sign. One must first have a clear idea of what he ought to be doing before he is apt to start doing it. Results show that the American history teacher probably is sensitive on this subject, is embarrassed to admit that he does not do all that he should by way of reading books and keeping abreast of latest scholarship.

Still, on another question most teachers indicated satisfaction that they read enough history. Twelve per cent reported that they read more than enough to teach their American history classes adequately, 47 per cent thought they read enough. Only 37 per cent admitted that they do not read as much as they should. Four per cent did not respond.

2. THE STUDENT

One often hears that high school students detest history. Not many American history teachers in Indiana accept such a gloomy estimate. But neither are they overly optimistic. Three per cent of the teachers did not respond to the question on student interest, and only 2 per cent thought their students had "very high" interest. Twenty-four per cent thought students had "high" interest, but 61 per cent considered student interest "average." Nine per cent saw their students as having "low" interest. Encouragingly, only 1 per cent thought students had "very low" interest in history.

The survey sought to discover the parts of American history preferred by students. As expected, teachers listed many topics and periods. The only topic drawing an overwhelming response was "war." Sixty-one per cent of the teachers either listed the topic "war" or one of the wars fought by the United States as a favorite subject of students. The only other part drawing a considerable response was "recent"—36 per cent of the teachers listing some part of recent American history as a favorite of their students. Other periods and topics—politics, colonial, economic—received scattered support. Viewed from broader perspective, teachers thought students far more interested in the Civil War and the period since the Civil War than those periods of American history up to 1860. Only 10 per cent of the teachers reported that students had major interest in periods before the Civil War. One must add, however, that 8 per cent did not respond to the question, and 36 per cent of the answers were not classifiable.

What parts of the subject do students dislike? Colonial history, according to teachers, is least popular. Nineteen per cent of the questionnaires noted colonial history among those parts liked least. Political history was next; it appeared on 14 per cent of the questionnaires. Though 42 per cent of the answers were not classifiable in broader categories, 28 per cent listed the period before the Civil War as the least popular part of the course, 14 per cent listed recent or post-1865 years.

On student ability, 43 per cent of the teachers thought their students had greater ability to memorize facts than to make generalizations from facts, 23 per cent thought student ability to make generalizations was higher. Thirty-one per cent saw no difference in students in this regard. Three per cent did not respond.

Regarding homework, there is an interesting situation. Only 4 per cent of the teachers reported assigning ten or more hours of reading weekly. Ninety-six per cent of Indiana's American history teachers calculated that they assign less than ten hours per week, 61 per cent figuring their assignments between three and five hours weekly. Such work hardly constitutes a great burden on the student, the more so because students can do much or all of it during the regular class hour in the period allotted to "supervised study."

On the question of ability grouping, 43 per cent of the teachers reported that their schools do not take into account individual differences in ability between students. Two per cent failed to respond, and 3 per cent did not explain the type of grouping in their schools. Thirty-six per cent reported that their schools grouped students by ability, while 16 per cent reported other types of grouping, principally grouping of individuals planning to go to college. Asked if they thought schools should do more in the way of taking into account student differences, a resounding 81 per cent responded "yes."

The survey sought information about students going to college. Twelve per cent of teachers made no response, 17 per cent estimated that fewer than 20 per cent of their American history students eventually go to college. The largest grouping was in the range from 20 to 49 per cent going to college—half the teachers reporting their students in that category. Only 21 per cent of the teachers reported that more than half their students find their way to college.

3. THE COURSE

The typical high school course in American history settles into a pattern that is partly chronological and partly topical, though more often the first than the second. Eighty-five per cent of those returning questionnaires stated that they combined the two methods of organization. If they follow their textbooks closely, they would do so. But a good many, 28 per cent, added that they dislike the present structure of the course, and an additional 17 per cent are not sufficiently satisfied to say expressly they wish no change.

At the moment there seems to be little sentiment to skip over the early period of history altogether. Ninety per cent of the teachers replied that they begin the subject with the colonial era or earlier, normally with the age of discovery. Some critics will say that this reveals why the course often does not come up to the present or even to the 1930's. Teachers, however, do not agree upon any one explanation of the difficulty. A variety of reasons occurred to them, but just 15 per cent thought the principal obstacle was too much material. Interestingly, only 4 per cent blamed themselves for proceeding too slowly.

Since so much of the course depends upon the textbook, it is important to know which one a school has adopted. The largest number, 30 per cent, reported they are using the venerable history written by David S. Muzzey. Despite repeated revisions this book inadequately reflects recent historical research. Nor is it likely to stimulate much student thinking. Nineteen per cent use the text by Canfield and Wilder; and 18 per cent, Bragdon and McCutchen—probably the best book on the list approved by the Indiana state textbook commission. Fourteen per cent do not use any of the approved books, a situation illustrating the degree of independent choice presently open to the individual school or teacher. Inasmuch as private schools are not obliged to select texts from the list, they would constitute some but not all those adopting unapproved books.

An American history course must rest upon much more than a textbook to deliver any substantial benefits. Thus a section of the questionnaire explored the character of the reading program. Sixty-eight per cent of the teachers reported that they require some kind of reading beyond the textbook. They indicated several ways of administering reading requirements: panel discussions, oral reports, written statements, term papers, or a combination of these. Though this is a rather impressive statistic, the success of any plan depends upon the quality of what students read and the manner in which the teacher integrates this activity with the course as a whole. In both respects firsthand observation reveals the need for improvement. Most of those who require reading ask everyone in their classes to do the work, whereas only 26 per cent require it of some students but not others. Teachers generally recognize that it is desirable for their students to read. And so the chief problem is how to accomplish that object.

4. THE CLASSROOM

Most teachers reported that they devote their class time to some combination of recitation, interpretative discussion, and lecturing. Seventy per cent said that they give about equal emphasis to recitation (short informational questions and answers) and interpretation, while the remainder either did not specify what they do or stated that they emphasize recitation. Naturally it is difficult even for the teacher to distinguish the two processes precisely and to indicate the level of thinking about a historical question. A majority, 66 per cent, lecture to their classes on occasion, but less than 40 per cent of the time. Those who lecture generally do so for part of a period because they find difficulty in maintaining student interest for fifty or so minutes straight.

As a rule, students spend part of the time in other ways. Seventy per cent of the teachers set aside a portion of the hour for supervised study, usually for reading the assignment in the textbook, though in some cases for work in the library. Only 5 per cent responded that they allot more than 40 per cent of the time for these purposes. In a good many schools there are no study periods, and so principals expect teachers to make such an arrangement. One consequence may be little or no homework.

Classroom activity revolves around examinations. It is the test that perennially worries the student and occupies much of the teacher's time, often more than he can reasonably afford. And yet when the student goes on to college, he seems ill-equipped to write clear, thoughtful papers in the essay examinations he usually faces. His instructor has the impression that he has never had to write this kind of answer previously. Replies to the questionnaire indicate that he has had more experience than his instructor realizes. In response to a query concerning the types of examinations they give, 84 per cent of the teachers, more than the authors would have estimated, said they include at least some essay questions in their tests. So only a small minority of students have taken "objective," true-false, multiple-choice, short-answer examinations and nothing else. Perhaps the trouble

lies in the infrequency with which teachers include
essay questions in examinations. The report by only 3
per cent of the teachers that they use exclusively essay
examinations suggests such an explanation.

As for current events, 70 per cent of the teachers replied that they include this activity in their
course. In correlating answers to different questions,
one finds that almost all teachers use magazines especially prepared for high school current events. Very
few assign anything beyond this kind of publication.
There are variations from the traditional practice of
spending each Friday on current events. Forty-six per
cent, however, have some sort of regular schedule,
and 33 per cent consider contemporary issues and events
when applicable to the work or interest of the students.

In answer to a question concerning materials em-
ployed in the course, 81 per cent said they use films,
but only 13 per cent bring them in as often as each
week or every other week. Fewer (53 per cent) show
film strips, and do so infrequently. Only one out of five
ever displays slides or conducts field trips, and then very
rarely. The average teacher therefore presides over a
course which is a truncated version of the "learning
experience" as defined by the progressive educationist.

In the past few years educational television has
carried American history to the classroom. Despite its
impressive growth and great promise, most schools have
not yet adopted ETV. Only 20 per cent of the teachers
said they receive television lectures in the course. And

while many did not express opinions about the value of this method of instruction, more disapproved (41 per cent) than approved it (33 per cent). In either case teachers recognize that TV lectures cannot replace or materially diminish their own role. Indeed if the program is effective, teachers have more rather than less to do.

5. THE LIBRARY

Several items on the librarian questionnaires concerned physical facilities. Fourteen per cent replied that there is no room set aside for a library. Indicative of pressures to use space for other purposes, only 57 per cent of the libraries operate as libraries every hour of the day, and 26 per cent serve also as study halls (for students reading textbooks) every period. A further pressure is the use of 43 per cent of the high school libraries by elementary as well as secondary students. Nineteen per cent of the libraries are less than six years old, demonstrating not only the extent of new construction but the problem of building new book collections as well. Sizable numbers of librarians in older schools think their facilities are inadequate; 51 per cent disapprove the size of the room; 20 per cent the adequacy of lighting; 31 per cent the extent of comfort; 56 per cent, the amount of privacy; 30 per cent, the degree of quiet. Although many students can use public libraries for materials unavailable at school, 48 per cent of them have to travel over two miles to do so.

In answer to a query asking how many volumes they hold in all subjects, 11 per cent of the librarians reported less than a thousand, 33 per cent between a thousand and three thousand, 31 per cent between three and five thousand, and 24 per cent over five thousand. But for books in American history—monographs, biographies, and sets—the totals are less impressive. Thirty-two per cent have less than one hundred volumes, 46 per cent have between one hundred and four hundred, and a slim 18 per cent have over four hundred. Some idea of the inadequacy of these holdings for high schools averaging several hundred students comes from the fact that one of the authors of the present volume has a personal library in history—mostly American history—of some four thousand volumes.

When the librarians checked a list of twenty basic books on American history to show those they have or are ordering, about 10 per cent said they have many of the items. The most popular book listed is Frederick Lewis Allen's *Only Yesterday* (34 per cent); and other leaders are Theodore White's *Making of the President, 1960* (32 per cent), Marquis James' *Andrew Jackson* (25 per cent), Benjamin Thomas's *Abraham Lincoln* (22 per cent), and Arthur M. Schlesinger, Jr.'s *Age of Roosevelt* (20 per cent). Only 5 per cent have some of the volumes in the *Chicago History of American Civilization Series*. Despite the arbitrary character of any such short list, the quality of most collections appears to be inferior.

A surprisingly large number of libraries, 61 per cent, have some paperback books, though many have been cautious about acquiring them in quantity. It is unusual for libraries to initiate or administer a program of selling paperbacks to students, but 31 per cent of the schools have book fairs, mainly operated by publishers and school officials or organizations.

To some extent, however limited it may be, teachers are asking students to use books in the library. Eighty-one per cent of the librarians said that the American history faculty have some requirements of this kind. Whether this would include all, some, or a few of the teachers and whether this means a substantial or a nominal amount of reading are areas difficult to explore by questionnaires sent to librarians. Further information on student reading appears in the foregoing section on the course.

To assure a systematic plan of purchasing new books, a library needs a definite budgetary allotment. Nevertheless 20 per cent either did not reply to the question whether they have such a budget or said they do not. Thirty-two per cent responded that their annual fund amounts to less than one thousand dollars, and fewer than 10 per cent have more than three thousand. An important point concerning budgets is the degree to which they are subject to expenditures for audiovisual materials. Fifty-one per cent reported a separate provision for this purpose, yet about half of these librarians failed to state how much audiovisual money they have.

Of those who did answer this part of the question, only 6 per cent indicated a sum of more than a thousand dollars.

The librarians' responses to an inquiry concerning the number of American history books ordered the previous year reveal a slow rate of expansion. Eighty-four per cent replied that they acquired less than forty books in the field, and about 20 per cent purchased less than five volumes. Though 82 per cent reported some participation by teachers in book selection, this may mean simply the opportunity to order rather than actual ordering. At least most teachers did not in fact order many volumes. In only 14 per cent of the cases did all the teachers in a school order over twenty books on American history. The librarians' count of books ordered appears incompatible with figures derived from the teacher questionnaires, for a third of the faculty estimated that they ordered ten books or more the previous year. This estimate seems too high.

6. THE OUTER WORLD

For one reason or another, as shown in Chapter 6, principals and other administrators do not have much personal involvement with the academic situation in the classroom. When asked if they were supervised too much, too little, or about the right amount, 76 per cent of the teachers answered that they had no complaints. A mere 1 per cent of the teachers said they were over-supervised. The preponderant number, 85 per cent, thought that administrators had at least a moderate or greater than moderate interest in what goes on inside the classroom. Yet 36 per cent replied that supervisors never visit their classes, and an additional 33 per cent reported that there were no more than one or two visits each year. Only one out of five have more than two visitors annually. If administrators are interested, they do not demonstrate it by looking in on their teachers, though some probably believe that visiting would be unjustifiable interference. One must conclude that their policy is beneficent *laissez-faire,* modified by occasional expressions of interest.

Parents are even less interested, say the teachers. Seventeen per cent of the respondents rated parental interest as greater than moderate, 40 per cent thought it was moderate, and 38 per cent described it as slight or nonexistent. Within the past few years parents have felt an increased concern about the educational progress of their children. Still they are reluctant to show it in their relations with educators unless a special problem arises. Teachers say they sometimes see the parents of poor high school students but hardly ever those of superior ones.

What measure of academic freedom do teachers have? In reply to a question whether administrators, civic groups, parents, or other teachers had ever advised them not to teach a certain topic, 6 per cent answered yes. Sometimes protesters may misunderstand what the teacher is doing, they may not view a sensitive topic in the context of the whole course, or their information about the matter may become garbled as it passes from person to person. To be sure, any restriction upon intelligent, dispassionate inquiry is too much, but the instances of real infringement of academic freedom are few.

★   INDEX

Ability grouping, 45–47, 62, 140
Abraham Lincoln: by Benjamin P. Thomas, 95, 147
Academic freedom, 125–26, 150–51
Activities: course projects, 62–64
Activities, extracurricular: of students, 48–50, 79–80; of teachers, 124, 134
Administrators, 102, 123; concern over American history course, 15–16; opinion of graduate degrees, 23; favor curriculum revision, 56; support of libraries, 100; often dominate P.T.A., 114–15; relations with school boards, 116–17; as obstacles to school reform, 120; and questionnaire survey, 125–26; and interest in history course, 149–50. *See also* principals *and* superintendents
Advanced credit examinations: at Indiana University, 40–43
Advanced placement program: expansion recommended, 60; test, 119

Age of Roosevelt, The: by Arthur M. Schlesinger, Jr., 147
Alexander Hamilton: by John C. Miller, 95
Allen, Frederick Lewis, 27; *Only Yesterday,* 25–26, 136, 147; *Since Yesterday,* 25–26
American Education Week, 115
American Heritage, 93
American Historical Association: teacher membership, 35; pamphlets, 66
American Nation Series, 98
American Observer, 85
American Statesmen Series, 92
Andrew Jackson: by Marquis James, 95, 147
Athletic coaches: as teachers of history, 17–19, 124, 131–32; often become principals, 109
Athletics: student distraction, 48–49
Atlantic Monthly, 94
Audiovisual aids and techniques, 17, 34, 62, 84, 88, 125; evaluation of, 86; and library funds, 100, 148–49

153

DATE DUE